A Brand New World

What Happens Next

by Jason Gastrich

A Brand New World

What Happens Next

These 44 stories were written between November 26, 2013 and August 18, 2014. *What Happens Next* is 93 pages long and the second book in *A Brand New World*. The first one is subtitled, *The First 15 Months* and it has 136 stories. See here: http://jasongastrich.com/mybooks.htm#abnw

The next book in *A Brand New World* is called, *The Fall*. I have already starting writing stories for it and I have many more story ideas in mind.

Remember. Things aren't always as they seem.

Sincerely,

Jason

A Brand New World:
What Happens Next

August 18, 2014 - A Bear With Benefits

August 17, 2014 - Cuckoo Ka Choo

August 13, 2014 - The Guber Meeting

August 12, 2014 - The Girl With Binoculars

August 10, 2014 - Pull Out and Invest

July 31, 2014 - Crack

July 29, 2014 - The Fever (Part 1)

July 20, 2014 - Rubber Valley

July 18, 2014 - Just In Case

July 12, 2014 - The Additive Weapon

May 26, 2014 - Worried Hate Assessment

May 18, 2014 - The Overserved Scheme

April 30, 2014 - Fit For Radio

April 29, 2014 - No Story, No Bad Press

April 28, 2014 - The Popularity Package

April 27, 2014 - The First GMO Oil

April 26, 2014 - Extra Supporters

April 25, 2014 - False Alarm

April 24, 2014 - The Abduction Scheme

April 23, 2014 - The Applicant We Know

April 22, 2014 - The Endorsement Deal

April 21, 2014 - Breathing Pain and Relief

April 20, 2014 - Here or There?

April 19, 2014 - Dog Gone It

March 23, 2014 - Ground Zero

February 19, 2014 - Black Sea Secrets

February 18, 2014 - The Veteran's Artificial Knee

February 17, 2014 - Business As Usual

January 24, 2014 - Her Reputation Revelation

January 5, 2014 - It's More Than a Game

December 20, 2013 - Exile Beats Execution

December 19, 2013 - Lend Me Your Ears

December 13, 2013 - The Thesis Experiment

December 9, 2013 - Just A Few Feet From Hell

December 8, 2013 - A Double Agent Defects (Part 2)

December 8, 2013 - Stupid Stealing

December 7, 2013 - Small Town Justice

December 6, 2013 - Another Third World Slaughter

December 6, 2013 - A Double Agent Defects (Part 1)

December 3, 2013 - Shape Changers

November 30, 2013 - Clean Freak

November 29, 2013 - Safety and Sacrifice

November 29, 2013 - Who's Who?

November 26, 2013 - Are the Lights On?

Are the Lights On?
November 26, 2013

"How many times have you done this?" Mack asked Captain Dave.

"This is the third year in a row. It is so relaxing. It's worth the risk, just to get away," Dave said.

"Ok. I'll go with you. It sounds like a plan. See you in the morning," Mack said to Dave.

The next day the guys flew 6,338 miles.

"For a small lie, it really pays off, you know?" Dave said and pointed to the lavish resort they were entering. It was like their own private paradise.

"Yeah, it's amazing here. The people are really nice, too. Are you sure they're not gonna find out back home?" Mack asked.

"Positive. All the news is monitored here under lock and key by the government and they've promised it's not coming out," Dan replied.

The next day the headline read, "Two Former FBI Agents Abducted in Iran" and they spent a cold, stuffy, snowy winter they would have spent with their in-laws in the warm, cheap and easy, 70-degree, sunny desert.

Who's Who?
November 29, 2013

Mark Leaf was almost finished ordering his medicine online. He had been using Goddess Delivers for a couple of years because they were fast and friendly. In fact, they would ship his order immediately and it would always arrive the next morning.

After Mark typed his address and credit card information, he pressed Submit, but it didn't work. It just stalled and acted like he didn't click Submit at all. Mark waited a few seconds and clicked Submit several times. After a long pause, like the computer was freezing up, it worked and went through. However, he didn't go to the typical redirect page where GD thanked him for his order. He was sent to a blank white page, but he didn't think much of it. He was just happy to have the money to order his medication. The state where he lived was too dumb and crooked to provide it.

Closing his browser, Mark opened his email and read the confirmation email GD sent him. It was confirmed. His medicine would be there in the morning! Since it was already 4:30 p.m., that was a pretty good deal, he thought.

Meanwhile, two spies were remotely watching his purchase on their computers. They had been spying on his computer for months and they knew where he purchased his medication. One of them wanted to give him poison and the other wanted to give him a boost.

Both spies arrived at the shipping location that night. After startling each other, they shot each other and died. They didn't even get a chance to use their medication that they spent copious amounts of time developing to look exactly like the real thing.

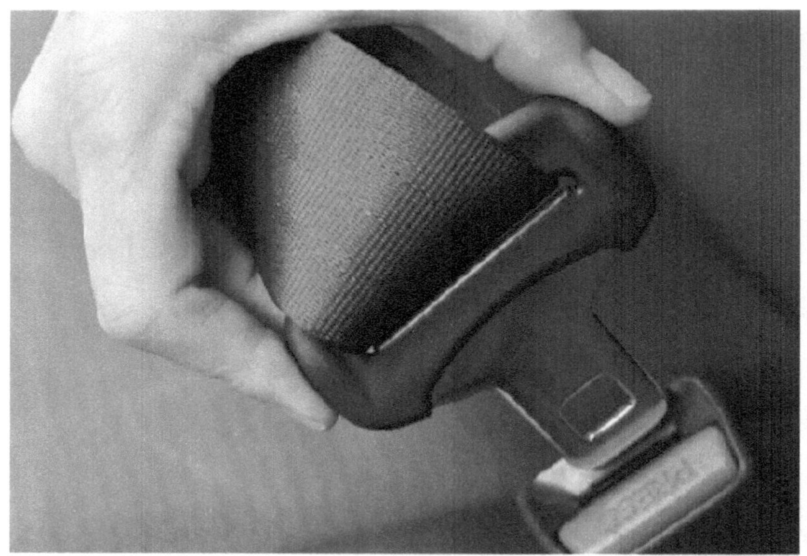

Safety and Sacrifice
November 29, 2013

"I'm starting to get some heat for this and you said I would be completely insulated. So, what's up? What do I gotta do, now?" the president said.

"Listen, it's not our fault you didn't want our safety feature. Maybe you should pass better safety laws, Mr. President," the GM representative said firmly and respectfully.

"You know those are tracking devices and so do I, so let's cut the bull," the president said.

The media was beginning to draw attention to the way Mexico bought cars from US manufacturers at a cheaper rate because they weren't including the safety feature. However, the safety feature included a computer system that would involve tracking the vehicle by satellite.

"And you know what else? So what if the roads don't have fancy lights or paint down the middle. My parents walked everywhere. They owned a donkey named Gus and a cow named Tahoe. That's it. Why don't you donate the money for our infrastructure?" he said.

"I don't know what else to tell you, but you might wanna buy the ones with the safety system. They can only help the function of the vehicle. You owe it to your people," the GM representative said.

"Listen, I know what's best for my people. You guys want to track and listen to the whole world. Well, we don't want any part of it. Go track yourself," the president said.

Clean Freak
November 30, 2013

"Congratulations to our first baby born underground!" the speaker said to thunderous applause from the large crowd who hadn't seen daylight in a decade.

Ahmed Ajin was a proud father and he worked very hard to make his country's clean energy program what it is today.

10 years ago, he wondered how he could ever leave regular society and live completely underground with his wife, but he didn't give it a second thought, today. He was a proud father and in more ways than one.

Shape Changers
December 3, 2013

"Ok, mommy, if you think so," Rachel said.

"Trust me. It will be for the best and you won't have to worry about it or think about it," Ruth replied.

"And you'll always have your roots, you know. You can change your face or your name, but you can never change who your family is," Rachel's dad said.

Rachel's mom and dad were very wealthy and they were moving to a prestigious neighborhood in Hollywood, California. They had planned to change Rachel's identity before they moved, so everyone in Hollywood would see them in a new way and she'd forget about her old self.

They were Jewish, but wanted to change their daughter's features and her name, so she wouldn't be stereotyped or discriminated against. They thought she'd have more opportunities if she blended in and they knew she'd still be given all of the Jewish privileges from certain casting directors.

"I have friends who can make sure your online profile never says you are Italian, German, Latino and Filipino. Sound good?" with a grin, Rachel's dad asked.

"Ok, daddy. I'll pretend I am those things. What will my new name be?" Rachel asked.

"Well, we can keep your first name, but we need to change your middle and last names. I'm open to suggestions. Let's see what your mother thinks," he said.

Before Ruth could reply, Rachel burst out and said, "I know! How about Rachel Anne Feldsteinberger!"

"No, that's too much like it is now," her mom replied.

"How about Rachel Ruth Ratzenberger!" Rachel exclaimed.

"Still too Jewish. How about Rachel Karen Franco?" her dad asked.

"Just Rachel Franco. I don't need a middle name," Rachel said, trying it on for size and deciding she liked it. "Rachel Franco. I could get used to that," she said.

"Great! I'll have my attorney file the legal paperwork and you have a plastic surgery appointment on Monday. Don't be afraid. They're just going to show you a video and talk to you," Rachel's dad reassured her.

"Ok. I like my nose, but I don't think I'll miss half of it at all," Rachel said as she crossed her eyes to see her nose. She had gotten teased by classmates as a kid and she had just gotten to the point where she didn't care a whole lot, but this seemed like an improvement to her.

"Maybe they can take the bone out of my nose and put it in my chin!" Rachel said.

"Maybe, but I don't think so. Talk to the doctor about a chin implant. Since you have an under bite, you might benefit from a chin implant," her dad said and she nodded her approval.

Later that night, after Rachel went to bed, her mom and dad were talking.

"What do you think about breast implants?" Ruth asked.

"For you or for Rachel?" dad asked.

"For Rachel, silly. I know you like mine," Ruth said and smiled. "Do you think she's too young or is this the right time?" she asked.

"12 years old is a little young. We should wait until she brings it up. Has she been bringing it up?" dad asked.

"Nope. Not really. Ok. I think you're right. She needs to get used to the other changes and everything. It will be a lot of stress for her, but she can do it. It'll be a fun change for all of us," she said and kissed dad good night and they went to sleep.

A Double Agent Defects (Part 1)
December 6, 2013

Abdul Al Hormuz had been detained at the Guantanamo Bay detention facility for six years. After initially speaking to an attorney, he wasn't given a trial or even a good explanation of his criminal charges.

Hormuz had been confined to a 15' x 15' jail cell with a toilet, sink and two others. He was from Saudi Arabia and the others were from Yemen. They were fed food they didn't like, but they were allowed to walk the yard twice a day and pray as they saw fit.

Today was the day America was cutting him a deal. His captors didn't know what to charge him with, where to give him a trial or what to do with him; which happened quite a bit.

At about 11 a.m., Hormuz was led into a chamber with a round table. The armed guard unlocked his handcuffs from behind his back and locked them in the front and to a leg of the table. He didn't change the cuffs on his feet, but he left Hormuz shackled, so he couldn't run anywhere if he got loose.

Captain Sean Kilpatrick of the United States Marines wanted to ask him some questions, so he arranged a meeting.

"Abdul, you don't wanna be here," Kilpatrick said. Fortunately, Hormuz had studied English and he was bilingual and understood.

"We want you to work for us. We'll let you go back to Saudi, but we want you to get involved with the network and let us know what's going on. We will pay you some now and some later, after you give us valuable information that proves to be true," the captain explained.

Hormuz's eyes widened. This was a tremendous offer. He could have his freedom and get paid. He only had to give some information and nobody would be able to confirm it or catch him again if they wanted to. It sounded like a win-win situation to him, so he said yes.

Within 48 hours, he was standing on an airstrip about to board an aircraft to fly back to Riyadh.

To be continued.

Another Third World Slaughter
December 6, 2013

In the year 2065, the South, Central and North American and Middle Eastern oil reserves were nearly depleted. The liquid petroleum and the natural gas was almost gone because the world was using it at a record rate, while the United States led the way.

There were oil reserves in Russia, but nobody was about to fight them for it. They also had huge reserves of iron ores, so they made all kinds of weapons and munitions.

In Africa, the oil was up for grabs. Sometimes, militias would overthrow the government and take oil fields. If you had weapons and an army, you could throw your hat in the ring, so to speak.

This time, the enemy was thinking more long term.

"I think they'll look the other way if we slaughter a few million people in Africa, bury them and come back and get the oil down the road. Look at this map. See this section here. It's small enough and dense enough, surrounded by desert, that we could get away with it," the president said.

"Yeah. We could do that. You really think nobody would step in?" the vice president asked.

"Well, someone might, but we could strike really fast. We could also make a political reason to get involved and do it there or in a neighboring country as a distraction. What other options do we have? We use 1,200 million barrels of oil a day and there is none left except for in Russia," he explained.

"Yeah, yeah. Ok. Well, should we do it alone or should we get another partner to help us?" he asked.

"France would do it with us. They have troops in Africa already," the president replied.

"Who do you think would come to their rescue, assuming the church stayed out of it?" he asked.

"I don't think anyone would. Egypt might, but we can scare them into not responding. It would slowly leak up the continent, but who would want to get involved? China? Russia? It's doubtful. The Arab League would stay out of it and the EU and UN would respond very slowly, if at all," he said.

"This is an awfully sick plan, though. Are you sure you can do this?"

"Well, there is already an overpopulation problem. These people are starving to death. It's almost humane. What else can we do? Do you think the planet was made to sustain 10 billion people like this?" he asked.

Small Town Justice
December 7, 2013

In a small Midwestern town, there was a kid who grew up holding grudges. He kept mental notes of everyone who wronged him, whether they said something mean, cut him off on the road, said something behind his back or whatever else might make him angry.

The kid grew up in the small town, knew everyone and eventually became the mayor, so he could teach a few lessons to people and he did. He used the Police force to be tougher on the people he didn't like and their children.

One day, the mayor was at a fair and it was clear he had been drinking alcohol. The Police officers were tired of doing his dirty work, so they gave him a quick sobriety test and took him to the station for being drunk in public.

"I didn't break any laws. You know. You don't have to stick me in here!" the mayor yelled as he sat handcuffed to a chair.

"We know, sir," the officer began.

"Don't call me sir and let's expedite this. I'm the mayor and I have a family to return to and a city to run," he said.

"You'll be treated just like everybody else. Since it's Friday afternoon, you'll be in the cell until you get arraigned on Monday. You'll see Judge Santos and he will set your bail. Just like everyone else. Okay?" the officer asked.

"You've got to be kidding me! Let me talk to your boss," he said.

"My boss already went home for the weekend. We can call him, if you like," the officer said to the mayor.

"Can't you just give me a citation?" the mayor asked.

"No, I can't. Rules are rules. We'd have to get the officer who arrested you to downgrade it, but he won't. I already know that. Just sit tight. You'll be arraigned and your bail will be very low. Something like $50,000," the officer explained.

"$50,000? That's outrageous," he exclaimed.

"Well, you can talk to the judge about that Monday. In the meantime, we'll give you a cot, a pillow and three meals a day. You'll have a shitter and that's about it. Okay?" the officer said and asked.

"Listen! When I get outta here, I'm gonna get justice. You sure you wanna go down this road?" the mayor asked.

"Sir, there's nothing else I can do. What would you like me to do?" he asked.

There was a long pause and a sigh. The mayor shook his head and didn't say a word.

Stupid Stealing
December 8, 2013

"Hey man! Look at that crane! Have you ever seen a truck with a crane like that on it, man!" Jose said to Juan.

"Wow! We could totally use it to cut palm trees! It would make it so much easier!" Juan exclaimed.

"Definitely, man. We wouldn't need the extra long cutters. We should steal it," Jose casually said and looked at Juan with a sly grin.

"Definitely. We definitely should. As soon as it gets dark, we'll come back and take it. I think that's like 30 minutes. I gotta go get my tools. Meet back here in 30 minutes. Okay?" Juan asked.

"Okay, homie. See you then. Don't be late. I'll bring a couple beers," Jose responded.

The two parted ways and in 30 minutes they returned to the same spot. Sitting behind a bush, across the street from the truck, they sat on the ground and quietly spoke.

"Here, take one, man. I brought Corona and there is some lime and a bottle opener in there. Let's do this!" Jose said.

"A man after my own heart," Juan replied and grabbed a beer, opened it, tossed a lime down the bottle's neck and took a sip.

After talking and drinking for a few minutes, they broke into the truck and drove off.

"Let's hit the freeway and get outta TJ, man," Juan said from the passenger seat, referring to Tijuana.

"We gotta get back to Mexico City asap. We have trees we gotta cut on Wednesday and we have about 1500 miles to drive," Jose reminded him. The streets would be dark and windy, too.

They were in Tijuana for the weekend on vacation visiting relatives and friends and they had to return to their home and tree cutting business in Mexico City. It would be a long drive and it would cost them a good deal in gasoline, but they had no other choice. They would have had to return by train or possibly in an overstuffed RV if their Uncle Raspberry was heading to Acapulco in time, but now they didn't have to worry about transportation.

They drove for two hours before they stopped at a gas station and convenience store. There wasn't much else around and dust blew down the dirty road as they pulled up. Juan needed to urinate and Jose wanted to buy some spicy peanuts. The truck had a half a tank of gas, so they didn't bother filling it, yet.

"See you in a minute, man," Jose said and walked inside the convenience store and bought some spicy peanuts. Juan noticed an odd cylinder in the back of the truck and had wanted to check it out, so he did.

Juan walked to the back of the truck and opened it. There was a round, white cylinder in the back and it looked like a propane tank for a gas grill. He knew those were explosive and he wanted to see if it was full or empty, so he grabbed it and pulled it out of the truck.

He noticed the cylinder was much heavier and awkward feeling than a propane tank. He also noticed something inside the tank. He shook it around a little and it bounced around and it made a clunking sound. Setting the tank on the ground, he opened the flap on the top and reached inside. There was another cylinder with weird white powder in it.

Pulling it out, he was amazed at its brilliance. It was like salt, only different. He poured some on his hands to feel what it was like and it burned. Juan dropped it immediately and rubbed it on his pants. It felt like ants were on him and then it felt like pins and needles sinking deep into his skin. The cylinder broke at his feet and spilled on his shoes, so his feet were tingling, too.

Right then, Jose returned.

"What is that stuff all over you, man?" Jose exclaimed. He looked like a ghost and he had white powder all over him and it was smelling funny because it was burning his skin and clothing. "You gotta get outta those clothes!" Jose exclaimed.

"You're right. I think this truck is cursed, man. We gotta get outta here fast," Juan said.

"I agree and you need a doctor, pronto. Let's at least get cleaned up and hit the night train," Jose replied.

The two went to a local church and showered. The couple who ran the church feed them carne asada and beans, then they hopped the train and headed south.

They slept in the back of the cargo train and as soon as they arrived in Mexico City, Juan went took the bus to the hospital and died from radiation poisoning within a few hours. He was exposed to cobalt-60. Jose didn't die, but his son Julio was born with a deformity from a mutated gene.

Julio was born with one normal ear and one that looked like a banana. He was also born with two toes that looked like pieces of rice and they eventually fell off.

A Double Agent Defects (Part 2)
December 8, 2013

Abdul Al Hormuz returned from Guantanamo Bay and there was a big celebration for him. His family and friends hadn't seen him in years, so they all wanted to congratulate him.

After the party ended and everyone went home, Hormuz took another shower and jumped in bed, but he had trouble sleeping.

One of his friends told him about a meeting he should go to in three days. In the basement of a mosque, about 200 people were assembling to discuss strategy. Every one of them represented others who wanted to invest in the group because they believed like them and supported their interests. This meeting was to discuss what they were going to do next and it was exactly the sort of information the US government wanted him to relay to them for the other half of the money.

Hormuz looked at the ceiling and he was lost in thought. His mind flashed back to childhood and his dreams about visiting Mecca and Medina on his hajj. He couldn't wait to be there with his friends and family and he fulfilled that dream when he was 18 years old.

Hormuz recalled college life and talking to friends about the United States. Some of them had a deep sympathy and love for the US, even though they didn't support their religion or their intervention. Most of them were hostile, but it was enough for Hormuz to take a different look at things.

After a couple of hours of deliberation, Hormuz drifted off to sleep. The next day he decided to go to the meeting and he did.

Hormuz got there early and went with his friend Az. They had known each other since they were 10 years old.

Sitting in the large crowd, they were about 20 feet from the front and in the middle. They could clearly see the speaker and he began to address everyone.

"Welcome everyone. Thank you for coming, tonight," the speaker said. Everyone clapped and cheered and gleefully sang, "Death to America! Death to the Jews! Death to America! Death to the Jews!" After about 10 minutes of singing this song, the bearded men dressed like Star Wars characters from Tatooine hugged each other and quieted down.

"We have been successful in Syria!" the speaker said to raucous cheering. "We are winning the war there and when Assad is toppled, we will be an integral part of the next government! We will get the oil fields and contracts this time!" the speaker said and everyone erupted in elation.

"Speaking of oil fields, there are more vulnerable oil fields in Africa we must take! They are in the hands of fools and unrepentant sinners and we need them for our purposes, not theirs!" the speaker announced and everyone agreed.

"We have some investors who want to sponsor a war on the new Benin oil field. It's almost operational and as soon as it is, I want us to be there. We can take it over and begin to take over the other ones, too," he explained and everyone cheered.

After some discussion about fees and donations, they prayed, embraced and left. Hormuz didn't feel like hanging out with his old friend, so he went for a walk.

He really didn't like either sentiment or option. On one hand, he could join the resistance movement and fight for the oil fields in Africa. They would likely put him in charge of a small squad.

On the other hand, he could tell Captain Kilpatrick their plans and get paid. Hormuz knew he could tell the captain nothing, a partial truth or the whole truth and he would never know the difference. However, if he waited to pay him until his lead resulted in arrests, he wouldn't get paid or have any more chances.

It all weighed on him a lot and he threw his arms up and looked up. He felt attached to his country, but he also felt like he had an obligation to the people who set him free. He decided to tell the captain a partial truth. He figured this would satisfy their requirements. It would give them a solid lead, so they could figure out the rest and it would net him $25,000.

The next day, Hormuz called Captain Kilpatrick on his cell phone from a quiet, secluded place and Hormuz told him how the network was planning to take over an oil field in northern Nigeria. The captain thanked him for the information and said the electronic funds transfer would take place as soon as they had confirmation.

Two weeks later, the network attacked the oil installation in Nigeria, but the Nigerian army was prepared and fended off the attack. They had been tipped off by the United States. The next day, Captain Kilpatrick authorized the funds transfer and Hormuz was paid. This was the last he ever heard from them.

Just A Few Feet From Hell
December 9, 2013

Moons and planets filled Ava's head with vivid pictures. She wondered how much time she should spend on him.

Chasing dreams was nothing new to Ava, but she didn't want to make a horrible mistake. She felt something inside for him and curiosity eventually overcame her power to resist. Since 10 was her lucky number, she finally decided to turn up on Tuesday the 10th at 10:10 a.m. and see him.

Ava spent Monday getting the courage to do it and she woke early Tuesday morning to get ready. She curled her hair and put on a little makeup. Ava wore something that could probably stop traffic, but she made it work and it didn't look slutty.

Ava told some friends something general about what she was doing, just so she'd feel safe. She knew it was an open campus and a public place, so she wasn't very worried. He had expressed interest for a couple of years, so she wanted to reciprocate and see if they were compatible and jump on him, so to speak, before anyone else could snatch him up.

At 9 a.m., she drove her car to Long Beach and parked in the student lot at Long Beach City College. It was about 10 a.m., so she got out of her car and paid the parking meter $1 and put the receipt on her dashboard. Grabbing her purse and sticking everything valuable under the seat, she exited her vehicle and felt really beautiful and confident because she was.

Entering the Viking food court, she noticed CNN playing in the corner and she figured he was nearby. She couldn't resist the coffee cart, so she ordered a cronut, which is a croissant crossed with a donut, and some coffee. The barista was friendly and almost a little off-put that someone so beautiful and friendly was there. She noticed her symmetrical features and she thought she had seen Ava somewhere.

After passing a beautiful girl at the cash register, she strutted across the lunch room and sat down in his view. Her back was toward him a little, though. She thought she'd make him work just a little to notice him. She also wanted to observe him. This seemed to work because it took about 15 minutes before he noticed who she was and he smiled. After their eyes met, he walked to her table.

CNN was playing a story about Iyanla Vanzant and her wonderful work encouraging people and holding them closely as they weep. They were praising her strong spirit and mentioning how she recently won an award for bravery.

Right as he was walking toward Ava, as two worlds were about to collide, the fire alarm went off. It was deafeningly loud and everyone froze. Holding their ears and awkwardly motioning to walk out, they left together and instinctually, almost like animals, made out like their ship was going down just a few feet from hell.

The Thesis Experiment
December 13, 2013

The only thing in between Alex and his Ph.D. was his thesis experiment. He had been working on his psychology degrees for 12 years and this was by far the most extravagant thing he ever tried. Alex was dressing like a 73-year-old woman for a poetry class. They were meeting at the local community college once a week in the afternoon.

Each week, Alex dressed up like a woman with the help of his friends. They took about 90 minutes to apply the makeup and fit the bodysuit. The body suit made him look about 60 pounds heavier. It was expensive and it was virtually impossible to tell it wasn't real.

For his thesis, he was writing about the way his classmates and teacher reacted to him as this woman. He noted how some people ignored him. Others treated him with scorn. Some paid a little special attention to him because they thought he was old and might need help. Alex even got away with parking in the handicapped zone because he walked slowly with a slight limp.

Alex's teacher didn't seem to realize the way the school recognized him as a man. He enrolled as one because that's what it says on his driver's license. Mr. Conley treated him like everyone else.

Mr. Conley was a poetry ninja. He could kill a poem and leap over a building in a single bound, but sometimes when he read his poetry it sounded a lot like free verse.

On the last week of class, Alex read his poem in Mr. Conley's class as a woman and everyone loved it.

Alex decided to never dress like a woman again after he accidentally saw an actual 73-year-old woman naked in the women's bathroom.

Lend Me Your Ears
December 19, 2013

Mark Reynolds sat in front of his computer and he wasn't sure what to think. He was one of Boeing's finest employees, but that had little to do with anything, now.

"Honey, this is really weird, but I think I'm supposed to listen to this guy," Mark said to his wife Chelsea, who was floating around the house in sweat pants.

"Really? What do you mean?" Chelsea asked.

"Well, after I graduated from Mein Coal College, Ric Lara found me a job at Boeing. Most of the companies paid him, but Boeing wasn't paying personnel agencies for some reason. He wouldn't take any money from me, like most headhunters would take a percentage as a fee. He just told me to listen to his son when he got older. That was like 25 years ago and this is him," Mark said pointing to the computer screen.

Chelsea looked at the computer and read some of the things Ric's son was saying. A puzzled look grew on her face.

"Wow. It sounds legit. What are you supposed to do?" Chelsea asked.

Mark and Chelsea didn't realize it, but Ric had made this request to many different people he placed in jobs around the country and the world. They started as entry-level employees, but most of them were in upper management, in highly technical computer fields, now.

"I guess the question I should ask myself is, 'What should I hear first?'" Mark said, clicking his mouse.

Exile Beats Execution
December 20, 2013

"How can I serve you, sir?" Jang Song-thaek graciously said to his younger superior, to whom he was related.

Kim Jong Un had called his uncle for a meeting.

"Sit down, please. Sit," Kim said, motioning to a chair.

"You've crossed the line one too many times. You're dreaming different dreams and we're going to put you down in the morning. You have a few hours to get your affairs in order," Kim said.

Before Song could respond, Kim's wife Lee Seol Ju stood up.

"No! He's your own flesh and blood. You can't execute him! Let him be exiled. We can tell everyone we executed him and he can never return, but don't kill him," Lee pleaded.

Kim loved Lee very much and ever since he married the rock star, he started having a more open mind. She really showed him the other half of life and everything he missed by being raised in such a strict, militant family.

"Are you sure about this? He is a traitor. We have a very good case against him. How can we trust him to truly disappear?" Kim asked.

Song stood up and spoke.

"Listen. I know I am from your father's regime. I am who I am and I can never change. I respect your decision to terminate me, but please let me go to the islands to live the rest of my days in solitude. I will stay away and you will never hear from me, again," Song promised.

This was a dilemma Kim hadn't anticipated. He thought it would be short and sweet and finished. However, he trusted his wife and decided to exile his uncle in secret.

The next day, Kim staged an execution and pretended to put Song to death. A man wearing a black hood on his head was given a lethal injection, but it wasn't really lethal. After getting the fake shot in the neck, the hooded figure slumped into his chair and played dead until they dropped the black curtain and stopped filming, then he took off the hood, stood and walked away.

Since the government controlled the media, it wasn't too difficult to get away with everything. Kim told the media his uncle was guilty of womanizing, treachery and corruption. Knowing how strict the communist regime was, nobody questioned the story.

Late that night, Song snuck away on a private jet. While he was flying, he had some surgery, liposuction and body sculpting surgery performed. By the time he landed, he looked and felt like a new man. For all intents and purposes, he was because he was starting a new life.

Song was given a new identity and his name was now Kim Lee Ji and he was from South Korea. He was to live on his savings and a small monthly stipend from the government and he was to be watched, so he could not return to North Korea or spread information about the regime.

It's More Than a Game
January 5, 20141

"Today, we're buying you some new shoes, son!" Richard Johnson said to his newly adopted son, Atem Apieth. Atem looked up at him and slowly nodded.

"I know everything is different here, but relax, have fun and be yourself. Ok?" Richard asked Atem and he nodded, again.

Atem arrived in the United States from Africa just three days earlier. He was from a war-torn town in South Sudan. The Johnson family had been on the foster family list for six months and since all-out war was about to break loose, African Adoptions expedited the adoption process. They flew Atem from South Sudan to Cairo to London to Los Angeles, where the Johnsons picked him up at the airport. He slept the next two days because of jet lag. Atem didn't sleep much as he traveled more than six thousand miles in two consecutive days.

"You're gonna do all kinds of fun stuff here in America, son. So, you're gonna need all different kinds of shoes. Ok? We'll get you some for running because I know you like to run," Richard said. Atem had participated in short, medium and long distance races and he was a fantastic runner with a very lean frame. He could run for hours without getting tired and it was where he'd think about life and relationships and everything under the sun.

"We'll get you some lightweight, supportive shoes for playing basketball, so you can shoot hoops. And we'll get you some casual shoes, too. Ok?" Richard explained and asked.

There was a pregnant pause, like he normally had lots of time to answer, then Atem answered.

"Yes, Mr. Johnson. Thank you. I understand. I'm just very tired," Atem explained.

"I totally understand, son. You had a very long flight and there is an 11-hour time difference between here and South Sudan," Richard explained.

"Ok. Let's get some new shoes!" Atem exclaimed and they drove to the local Sports Authority store. In his village, some kids didn't have shoes, so he only owned one pair for wearing out and one for bathing.

Sports Authority had all kinds of shoes from bicycling to running to baseball to football to soccer to track. They also sold casual shoes, tennis shoes and an assortment of sandals, equipment and other stuff.

"How can we help you guys, today?" Sheila Shakuka the sales associated asked.

"We're looking for some running shoes, some basketball shoes and some casual shoes for Atem here," Richard said with a smile to Sheila.

"Ok. Let's start by measuring his feet," she said as she pulled out a measuring device. Atem removed his shoes and socks, so she could measure his feet and they were size 8. His feet were large for his age, so he was probably going to be a tall man one day.

"Take a seat, Atem. Let me show you this video. It will explain everything you ever needed to know about shoes to you," Sheila said. For the next 15 minutes, they watched an amazing video presentation and popular, professional and college athletes demonstrated how different shoes helped them play sports. The inspirational video focused on popular brands and it made Atem excited about finding some great shoes to wear while playing his favorite sports.

"You're a size 8, so let's talk running shoes. What kind of surface do you usually run on? You know, do you prefer running on grass, on pavement or indoors?" Sheila asked him.

Atem thought for a few seconds and replied.

"I will run on anything. I like running on dirt or short grass," he explained. Sheila seemed to know exactly what he needed. She found a pair of running shoes in his size, handed them to him and he loved them. After trying the shoes on, he was so excited, he wouldn't stop walking and jumping until they asked him to calm down.

"Ok, so those are yours. I know you really like them, but let's take them off now and check out some basketball shoes," Richard said and Atem did what he was told.

"Which position do you play in basketball? Do you like center or guard or forward?" Sheila asked Atem.

"I play anything. I dribble a lot and I'm very quick," he explained.

"Ok, it sounds like you'd play guard. You'll want something lightweight like these," she said and found some black high tops, quickly laced them and handed the shoes to him. Just like last time, he wouldn't take the shoes off until he was asked. He found a basketball and dribbled it around the store. Eventually, they were able to corral him.

"Ok, well, I can see you really like those ones, too! So, we'll get you those. Now, let's take a look at some casual shoes you can wear around the house or out with your friends," Richard said.

"Ok, Mr. Johnson," Atem said.

"Which sort of activities will you be doing? Will you do much walking or do you just want something to wear to the shopping mall and to dinner?" Sheila asked.

"I might need one shoe for dinner and another shoe for walking and the mall," Atem replied and looked at Mr. Johnson.

"No problem. We can buy you four pairs. Show him one for dining and another for hanging out with friends at the mall, please," Richard said to Sheila, who smiled and said ok.

Atem tried on a few different pairs of shoes because the first ones hurt his feet. Eventually, he found a pair of shoes for nice dinners and another pair for hanging out with friends.

Meanwhile, on the other side of the world, two very powerful men were about to meet. These men had discussed meeting for a while and today was the big day. Abdullah Al Assad was finally meeting Vladimir Smirnoff in his new office to discuss business.

Vladimir's secretary led Abdullah through another room with a vaulted ceiling and into Vladimir's office where he and the minister of war were talking.

"Mr. Smirnoff, Mr. Al Assad is here to see you," the secretary said and they approached each other, exchanged pleasantries and shook hands.

"And I'd like you to meet my war minister. His name is Adolf Lenin and he can explain to us exactly what you need," Vladimir said.

Adolf was prepared for this moment. He researched every hill and every valley on the battlefield. He had built a model to illustrate which weapons could be used to do the most damage. He also knew the rebels' capabilities and which weapons Al Assad needed to repel.

The war had become a game of sorts because Adolf had to figure out which weapons they needed and where they needed to use them to win. Why? Living people buy a lot more weapons than dead people. If they were to win battles, they would buy more weapons and ammunition. This symbiotic relationship made them allies.

During the past few years, Al Assad bought weapons and ammunition from Smirnoff and it helped his armies fight terrorists and protect his ancient land. As technology advanced, he upgraded his orders to keep up with his enemies. However, recently certain terrorists were fighting him with very advanced weaponry. Al Assad's men needed anti-aircraft missiles, tanks, jets, machine guns, helicopters and a little luck.

"Please look at the screen!" Adolf said and pointed to a 120" HD TV on the wall. In stereo sound, they watched in awe as a black helicopter flew in all directions, shooting things, causing explosions and mayhem and then the camera would pan to Adolf and Smirnoff and they were laughing, wearing funny hats in the snow.

"Did you like that?" Adolf asked. Al Assad's mouth was getting dry from gaping open and he could only nod his approval. "Well, check out this," he said and continued the video.

This time they watched ten tanks roll into a village and completely destroy it. It was a real life video, too. People were screaming, running and being killed. The tanks did a fantastic job of destroying all the structures and it looked like many people of indiscernible descent were killed.

Al Assad turned to Adolf and Smirnoff and they wore reserved smiles. They all watched the destruction like they knew it had to happen. Every so often, one of them would nod or point at the screen and talk about the weaponry or the chaos. It was a remote village the Russians cleared out because they wanted it for its oil reserves.

"How well do your anti-aircraft missiles work? Do they have tracking? Are we talking 100% or what?" Al Assad asked.

"We're glad you asked!" Adolf exclaimed.

"Here. Watch this," Smirnoff said as fast forwarded the video a few minutes. The screen showed a man with an anti-aircraft gun over his shoulder. As a plane was flying overhead, he fired the weapon and it hit its target. Although they couldn't see the plane crash, smoke rose from its fuselage and as it flew lower and lower into the distance, they knew it was going to crash, soon.

"Excellent. I'll take it all. Thank you," Al Assad said and it was so.

Her Reputation Revelation
January 24, 2014

As Toni approached the reputation monitoring company, she smiled. This was a unique opportunity to rate her image and improve it.

"I'm a little nervous," she said to her boyfriend Johnny.

"Don't worry. These guys come highly recommended. I know this is an outside of the box sort of thing, but the top celebs like Ed Helms and Dane Cook are doin' it and I think it's a great idea," Johnny said.

"Ok. I'll trust your judgment because I really don't know," Toni said.

Parking her electric car in the parking lot, Toni and Johnny walked into the building.

"Welcome to Five Star Reputations! I'm Gloria and I'm going to be your host, today. Would you guys like something to drink?" she asked.

"Sure!" they said in unison. Gloria walked to the refrigerator, grabbed two water bottles and handed the water to them and asked Toni and Gloria to sit on the leather sofa.

"You're going to be excited when I explain the program to you. And you have a couple of options, so let me know if you have any questions. Just interrupt me whenever you want. Ok?" Gloria explained and asked and Toni and Johnny affirmatively nodded.

"The two options I have for you are the Gold package and the Platinum package. I'll explain the Gold one first. With the Gold package, you get 10 hours of look-alike status reports. We send professionally dressed look-alikes into the general public and we gauge people's reactions to them. We do this with hidden cameras, so we know exactly what people are thinking about you and how they would respond if it were really you. We'll give you a detailed report, citing incidents of indifference, looks of endearment, pointing, calling their friends to tell them they spotted you and things of that nature," Gloria said.

"Hidden cameras? Wow. How do you do that?" Johnny asked.

"Each look-alike wears tiny video cameras the size of a pinhead and they capture everything really well," Gloria replied.

"What if someone asks one of the look-alikes if they're me? What will they say or do?" Toni asked.

"When that happens, they politely say no and we let you know," Gloria said and continued. "In addition to the 10 hour analysis and report, we will give you a detailed web report about your online reputation. Are people talking about you? If so, what are they saying? What is the ratio of positive things to negative things? Where are people talking about you? The report will answer all of those questions and give other details about your current reputation," Gloria said.

"Ok. That sounds great," Toni said.

"What's in the Platinum package?" Johnny asked.

"The Platinum package is everything in the Gold package, plus a couple more things. It includes 20 hours of look-alike status reports and it also includes our trademarked Reputation Recommendation report. This special report is 10 pages long and it will give you about 40 different ways you can improve your reputation or your brand. Based on the status reports, our computer software and one of our analysts will produce a detailed report for you," Gloria explained.

"Ok. I think I want the Platinum package. How much is it?" Toni asked.

"We have two payment options. If you pay up front, it's $999. If you break it into three monthly payments, it costs $1199," Gloria replied.

"Sounds great. I'll pay you up front. Do you take Visa?" she asked.

Business As Usual
February 17, 2014

"Please come in, Mr. Dong," the secretary said to the Chinese vice president. Dong was finally meeting Mr. Sun, today. They had very important business matters to discuss.

As Dong entered, he noticed Sun's medals, diplomas and trophies. Before he became prime minister, he was a decorated war veteran, highly educated and played many sports. He did everything very well, too.

"Hello, sir," he said and shook hands with his old friend. They had met many times and talked on the phone about various private, political and social matters.

"Hello, Sun. How are you?" Dong asked.

"I am good. Please sit. I don't have much time and we need to talk," Sun said.

"Yes. I cannot wait to continue our work," Dong said and sat on a square mat on the floor. Sun followed his lead and sat on another mat facing Dong. A warm cup of organic green tea was beside each of them and they took a small sip.

They had been secretly poisoning their enemies for years. This meeting was to discuss how they could continue their work and do it even better.

"You know that Easy Sleazy doll we manufacture? Well, our scientists have developed poison that is undetectable by current, detection systems," Sun said.

"That's fantastic! Where are you shipping them?" Dong inquired.

"We will begin shipping them to the United States and Japan in two weeks," Sun proudly declared.

"Very good. Guess what we have developed," Dong instructed.

"Did you finally manage to lace the iPhone with poison?" Sun asked and they both laughed hysterically until tears filled their eyes and their cheeks hurt. Several minutes later, Dong and Sun regained their composure and continued.

"You know we're working on that, but we have something even bigger in mind," Dong proudly announced.

TO BE CONTINUED

The Veteran's Artificial Knee
February 18, 2014

As Casey walked toward the airport's security scanner, a frown fell on his face. He knew his artificial knee was going to set it off.

"Hello, sir. Do you have any metal in your pockets?" the TSA agent wielding a plastic wand said.

"No, not in my pockets," Casey replied.

"Ok, please walk through," the agent said and gestured to an 8' tall security scanner. As Casey obeyed, the scanner beeped, indicating he had something metal.

"Please come back and walk through, again," the agent instructed. Casey walked back and walked through again, but it beeped, again.

"Come here, sir. We have to take you into a room and strip search you," the agent said.

"Are you serious? C'mon. I have a plane to catch and I don't have anything dangerous or illegal. I'll tell you what I do have, though. My knee was damaged in Vietnam and they had to replace it. Now, it always sets these things off," Casey explained.

The agent seemed to believe him, but his word wasn't good enough, so he apologized for the inconvenience and took him into a room and strip searched him.

300 miles away, in a brightly lit control center, another government agent was examining Casey. Unknown to him and nearly everyone else, the knee replacement contained a GPS device, so they always knew where he went. They did this because Casey was wounded in battle and killed some people in the war, so they weren't sure where he would go or what he would do after he returned to regular society at home. Some war veterans were unable to adjust and moved to the mountains and tuned out or became a danger to themselves and others.

Not only did the artificial knee transmit his location to a satellite, but it also sent other details like his heart rate, body temperature and blood pressure. In fact, the computer had a detailed report of the places he went during the past four decades and how his body responded to each environment.

Black Sea Secrets
February 19, 2014

Six Weeks Ago in Washington, D.C.

"General Samson, Vladimir Vitko is on the phone for you, sir," Samson's aide said with one hand on the receiver.

"I'll take it in my office," Samson said, closing his office door. "Hello, Vlad?" he said into his phone.

"Yes, how are you doing, Mr. Samson?" Vitko asked.

"I'm well. You can call me John, Vlad. We've known each other long enough, my friend," Samson said. They had spoken on several occasions during the past three years and they met once in Geneva.

"Are you and your crew still coming for the Olympics?" Vitko asked.

"Of course. We wouldn't miss it for the world. I'm navigating one of our newest destroyers there, too. You'll have to come onboard and I'll show you around. It's a truly amazing vessel with unparalleled radar technology," Samson raved.

Today in Sochi, Russia

"It's just going to be you and me, okay. You will have six of these and I want you to stick them in six different places throughout the ship," Vitko said handing his young comrade Sergei the tiny devices. Sergei was hired and trained for this important and risky mission.

"Yes, of course. Nobody will ever know what I'm doing because I will do it when they are not watching me. Even where there are cameras, I have ways to quickly and quietly attach the listening and monitoring devices, so they will not see me," Sergei said. He had been given a map of the ship and he studied it, so he knew where everything was located.

"Very good. They have invited me to tour the USS Chung-Wang, tomorrow, at 0600 hours, so be ready. You are coming with me," Samson said.

"Yes, sir. I was born ready," Sergei replied.

Samson and Sergei boarded the American vessel the next day and Sergei planted all of the devices. They wore tiny, undetectable cameras and photographed most of the ship, too. The listening and tracking devices were designed to fly under the radar while transmitting information to a Russian satellite, so they could monitor the latest technology and understand how it was being used. They were also able to hear the seamen's conversations.

Ground Zero
March 23, 2014

"I don't know if we can handle another scandal, sir," the prime minister's bright aide said with open palms. During the past year, his reputation had been tarnished for violating people's rights and censoring the media and the Internet. In one week, he was seeking reelection.

"Listen. The people want me to be their leader, so I am going to lead," the prime minister authoritatively replied.

"Okay, well, the minister of war is here to see you, sir," the aide said.

"Send him in," the prime minister replied and sat in the padded chair behind his cedar desk.

A tan, tall man with a gray beard entered and sat in the chair in front of the prime minister's desk.

"If they enter our airspace, I want you to shoot them down. Do you understand me?" the primer minister instructed and asked with an impenetrable stare.

"Yes, sir. What if it's over a populated area?" he asked.

"Shoot it down before it gets to a populated area," the prime minister quickly replied.

"Yes, sir. If they enter our airspace, we will down them, immediately. Is there anything else?" he asked.

"That's it. Thank you," the prime minister said and the war minister quickly left.

Two days later, it happened.

Inside the military's border region control room, a bright blip was moving on the radar screen.

"Sir, we've spotted a plane about to enter our airspace from the south," the lieutenant announced to the crew in the room and specifically the commander.

"Ready the surface-to-air missiles, lieutenant," the commander said.

"Yes, sir," the lieutenant replied. The missile operators answered the call and they were ready in three minutes. The lieutenant told the commander and he gave orders to fire at will and they did.

The first missile missed its target and landed in an abandoned field. The second missile tore through the warplane's aluminum wing and sent it spinning. The pilot ejected and a few seconds later, his parachute opened and he floated to the ground.

The plane continued flying about 200 yards and crashed into a water treatment plant. It was the only water treatment plant in the country and it processed sewage and filtered household and drinking water for cities.

When the plane crashed, it caused a large explosion because it was full of fuel. The fire department raced to the scene and it took them six hours to put out the 40-foot flames. By the time they were finished, all of the firefighters felt sick and some of them fell unconscious. An ambulance arrived about 30 minutes later and doctors treated the injured people and took them to the hospital.

In the light the next day, investigators determined that the plane wasn't just filled with jet fuel, but it was also filled with radioactive material. The water treatment plant was ground zero.

Dog Gone It
April 19, 2014

As Terry and Brendon approached the white mansion, they were dressed in black from head to toe. This was the golden opportunity they had been waiting a long time for.

Terry and Brendon had been casing a $10 million mansion in California's Hollywood Hills for nine months. They knew the entire family was out of town on vacation, so they came to steal their money and valuables. Not only did they know the family was gone, but they knew a lot about the mansion's layout.

During his time in prison, Terry met a home alarm specialist named Julio. Julio broke into a database and discovered all sorts of details about the alarm company the family was using and told Terry, so he could learn how to turn it off. On the Internet, Terry found some thieves discussing a flaw in the alarm and it worked. He punched the override code into the box and it disabled the alarm.

"Do you think you can hop the gate?" Terry asked Brendon. The automatic gate was metal, but painted to look like wood. It was about eight feet high in the middle and ten feet high on the sides. The gate was quite grandiose.

"No problem," Brendon said and flung himself over the locked gate like he had done it before. Terry quickly followed. Once they were on the other side, they walked the long and windy driveway to the mansion's front door.

"I hope I can pick the locks. Let me get started," Terry said. He opened his lock pick bag and took out his expensive set of professional lock picks.

Terry had been trained by the US army to pick locks. He spent 12 years in the service and had many opportunities to pick locks, so he was very good at it. After leaving the military, he worked for a locksmith in a hardware store for eight years.

Brendon looked around the corner of the mansion and the motion light came on. Since nobody was home and since the house was on a secluded hill, they weren't too worried about the light. Everyone knows animals and bugs set them off.

Since he had to pick a doorknob lock and two bolt locks, it took about 20 minutes. Eventually, the large door popped open and they entered.

Terry and Brendon stood in the vaulted entrance to the one-acre home that was sitting on three acres of expensive land. The home was recently built, so everything looked and smelled brand new. They wanted to work fast because they didn't know if the mansion had any other security devices or if neighbors, family or friends might visit to check on it for the owner.

Terry had bitten into the security cameras throughout the mansion, so he knew where everything was. Using a scanner and sitting in his van, he could see and record everything the cameras caught on film.

They weren't very concerned about the recording because all you could see was their eyes. They both wore the same black garb from head to toe, so their skin was concealed and they were almost indiscernible from each other. The only details the camera could convey were a rough height and weight.

Before they got far, a sweet black dog with a red collar approached them. It was the sweetest thing they had ever seen and it couldn't have been more than six months old.

"So this is what she looks like. I saw her on the CCT video, but I couldn't tell how big she was. Aww. Come here, girl. What does her chain say?" Terry asked.

Brendon slowly put one hand on the dog's collar and the other hand turned the nametag over and it said, "Queen Vanessa".

"C'mon. Let's do the job and I know which room has no cameras and we can grab some beers and play with the dog for a minute," Terry said.

"Fine. Then we're outta here. Let's make this quick," Brendon said as they hurried down the hallway and sacked the house.

After looting the valuables in the mansion, Terry opened the refrigerator and found two beers. He gave one to Brendon and motioned to him to follow him and he did. Vanessa followed, too.

"Come on. This room has no cameras. I noticed earlier there's a TV and a pool table in it. Check it out," Terry said, picking up a pool stick and handing Brendon a cold beer.

"Wow, this is a rad dog," Brendon said, petting Vanessa.

The guys wanted to leave as quickly as possible, but they didn't mind spending five minutes drinking a beer in the pool room. Their thick clothes made them work up a sweat, so it cooled them off. The dog loved being with them, too.

They took off their ski caps and scarves, since there weren't any cameras. Both of them played with Vanessa for a minute or two, letting her lick their faces and roughhouse a little.

"Alright. Let's get outta here. This place is starting to creep me out," Brendon said.

"You're right. Let's go," Terry said and they walked to the gate, hopped it and drove away.

When the family came home, Mr. Walters noticed some of his belongings were missing. He checked the security cameras and saw two men in black, stealing money, jewelry and other valuables throughout his home.

After watching the entire video, he sat down in front of his computer and launched the Dog Sight application. The application was also on his cell phone, but he wanted to make sure he saved a copy to his computer, too.

Through the tiny camera in Vanessa's eyeball, he was able to capture the criminal's faces in living color and high definition. In fact, since they played with Vanessa, he had a few minutes of fantastic video that the police used to find and arrest Terry and Brendon.

Here or There?
April 20, 2014

As Ahmed sat in the large, white tent with his laptop computer, he was nervous and scared of a drone attack. His satellite Internet connection was very good, even though he was in the hot, dry Rub' al Khali desert. It was even encrypted, so nobody else could see or track the transmission.

Ahmed was about to receive a transmission to broadcast live on the Internet. Hundreds of miles away, his friends were enjoying a big picnic because some prisoners they knew and loved were finally set free. It was a little like a pep rally.

"Praise Allah because we have our friends back!" Muhammad said and everyone cheered, kissed each other on the cheek, pumped their fists in the air and chanted.

"We will settle the score soon. They can run, but they cannot hide!" Muhammad yelled and everyone cheered and chanted again.

"Listen! They can build their weapons of mass destruction and threaten us, but we have something they don't. Our secret weapons!" Muhammad screamed and everyone hugged each other, smiled and laughed.

Ali wanted to have fun at the picnic, but he was working. He was filming it with a video camera and streaming it to Ahmed's computer in another part of Yemen's Rub' al Khali desert.

The picnic lasted about six hours. Many devout and radical Muslims ate, drank and chanted all sorts of things. It was quite a scene and it was sent to Ahmed who broadcasted it live online. While he was broadcasting it in real time, his little brother yelled to him from outside the tent. He said he saw smoke, so Ahmed ran outside to see it.

About a mile away, black smoke was rising from the local trash repository. It was being stored in a big white tent just like the ones Ahmed and Ali were in. Fortunately, no people were inside the trash tent.

"Look, Ahmed!" the little boy yelled and pointed to a moving dot in the big blue sky.

"An attack drone! C'mon! Let's get back inside!" he said and they quickly reentered the tent.

Ahmed smiled and emailed Ali. It said, "They bought it. Operation: Burn Our Trash, Accomplished."

Ahmed broadcasted the picnic, but he had also hacked the attack drone's computer and video feed, making it think its missiles and machine guns hit his tent when it really destroyed the trash tent about a mile away.

Breathing Pain and Relief
April 21, 2014

Saturday night's cool, crisp air on the New Jersey boardwalk smelled clean. The sun had set hours ago, but they could hear the small waves gently crashing on the shore.

Ronald and Phillip were meeting James and Morris about their new business idea in their corporate office. It was small, but very nice and it had a beautiful view.

They had been selling cigarettes to Americans and the rest of the world for five decades and they were heirs to the company and began working for it at a young age. Since their grandparents founded the company, they were set for life, but their grandparents and parents had passed away, so it belonged to them now.

"Is the bar still stocked?" Ronald expectantly asked James.

"Yeah, but let's hash out some business first," James replied and motioned to Ronald to sit.

"Okay, well, I don't have all night and I'd like to have a drink, so let's sit down and do this," Ronald said. The others obliged and they all sat in new chairs around a round table.

"I know it's a radical move, but I think it's time we stop advertising cigarettes and use our resources elsewhere. We've been spending $24 million a day," Morris said.

"Okay, but what will we do with it? If we don't have a better investment plan, then why change things?" Phillip asked.

James and Morris had discussed the new idea before the meeting, so they were on the same page.

"Marijuana. Marijuana is the way to keep our business relevant throughout the 21st century," James said.

"Do you guys remember what my dad said before he passed away?" Morris asked. Nobody said anything. "My dad said we were selling a disease and it would be a burden until we sold the cure," Morris explained.

A hush fell on the room. All of the guys actually did remember him saying that now.

"Okay. I'm listening. What's your plan?" Phillip asked.

For the next two hours, they discussed growing, harvesting and selling marijuana. They cited studies where it stopped cancerous growths. Some of them raved about how great it was from their personal experience. They also mentioned how it was legalized for recreational use in Colorado and Washington and for medical use in many other states. Phillip cited how it was decriminalized or legal in several countries. James mentioned the Marijuana Policy Project and their efforts and network.

"I don't think we can go wrong with this one. Let's start growing cannabis in Colorado and Washington. We will invest in some fields and some processing plants and it will be a great test before we go nationwide for the medical cannabis market and eventually worldwide where it's legal," Morris said.

Everyone agreed.

The Endorsement Deal
April 22, 2014

"Mrs. Gorbush, Senator Throttlebush is here to see you," the secretary said through the receiver.

"Okay. Please send her in," Mrs. Gorbush said, hanging up the phone in her office and standing to meet her. Today was an important day and this was an important meeting.

"It's good to see you! How have you been?" Mrs. Gorbush asked.

"I'm fine. Thank you. How are you?" Senator Throttlebush asked.

"I'm well. Please sit down," Mrs. Gorbush said, motioning to the brown chair in front of her big, oak desk. Senator Throttlebush sat, crossed her ankles and folded her hands on her lap.

"Thanks for entertaining our offer. We actually have three packages from you to choose from, so check them out and let me know which one you prefer," Mrs. Gorbush said and Mrs. Throttlebush nodded as she accepted three cards.

One card was bronze and $40,000 was written in big type on the top. There was one paragraph below it that read:

"I agree to endorse Mrs. Gorbush for United States president and I will write a press release stating my unequivocal endorsement."

Below this statement was a place for her to print and sign her name.

The next card was silver and $50,000 was written in big type on the top. It read:

"I agree to endorse Mrs. Gorbush for United States president and I will write a press release stating my unequivocal endorsement. I also agree to campaign with Mrs. Gorbush on July 10, 2015 in Seattle, Washington. Below this statement was a place for her to print and sign her name.

Since Senator Throttlebush was a Washington senator, Mrs. Gorbush's campaign wanted to pay her to come to her upcoming campaign rally in Seattle. If the senator's constituents and supporters would vote for Mrs. Gorbush in 2016, it could help her win the state of Washington and possibly even the presidential election.

The third card was gold and $75,000 was written in big type on top. It read:

"I agree to endorse Mrs. Gorbush for United States president and I will write a press release stating my unequivocal endorsement. I also agree to campaign with Mrs. Gorbush on July 10, 2015, in Seattle, Washington.

I agree to contact my constituents and followers on Facebook, Twitter, by email and on one page on my website, endorsing Mrs. Gorbush's presidential campaign until the 2016 presidential election. Below this statement was a place for her to print and sign her name.

After she had read and considered each card's offer, Mrs. Gorbush asked the senator if she had any questions.

"No. I understand. I'm having second thoughts, though. This feels a little unethical. Am I wrong?" the senator asked.

"No. I think it's only unethical if you don't think I would make the best president," Mrs. Gorbush replied.

"Okay. Well, I guess I'll see you in Seattle!" Mrs. Throttlebush said.

The Applicant We Know
April 23, 2014

"I really liked Tom DeVey a lot. I think he interviewed very well and he earned his Master's degree in Business Administration at Harvard University," Robert Smith, the company's top recruiter said. They needed to fill 18 positions, but this was the most important one because it was for the new Chief Financial Officer (CFO).

"I liked him, too. How about Rick Ruben?" Dr. S. Johansson said.

"Rick was pretty good. I liked his credentials and everything. He seemed to really understand and enjoy our product line, so we won't have to spend too much time training him," Smith said.

"Very well. Are there any other notable candidates?" Johansson asked.

"Not really. Those two guys are definitely the ones we want to consider," Smith said.

"Okay. Let me have their files and I will make the final decision. Thanks for your hard work," Johansson said, shaking Smith's hand.

"It was my pleasure, sir. Let me know if you have any questions and I'll continue working to fill the other positions," Smith said as he left Johansson's office.

Dr. Johansson put the files on his desk and gazed at his computer screen. Moving his mouse, his system left hibernation and he launched the Inside Info application on his desktop.

Typing Tom DeVey's name into the box, he clicked search and the software looked for all sorts of information about DeVey. Unfortunately, it couldn't find much. It said he frequently visits news websites, emails his daughter and girlfriend, uses Twitter daily and is a registered voter without a political party.

Typing Rick Ruben's name into the box, he clicked search and a few details came up. It showed 12 porn websites Ruben liked to visit. He was $40,000 in debt and declared bankruptcy a few years ago and he was recently on trial for manslaughter. It also said he was a member of the Ku Klux Klan.

Johansson clicked a link that wasn't available on DeLey's profile to obtain even more information about Ruben and it took a minute to retrieve it. This link gave him all sorts of information like all of his previous residences and employers, net worth, bank account information, driving record, arrest record and medical history.

Johansson spent about an hour reviewing everything and decided he wasn't the best candidate for the company. Although some of the porn was alarming, his driving record and arrest record were the most disturbing aspects of his profile.

The next day, Dr. Johansson called Smith's office.

"Hey Robert. I decided to go with Rick, so could you please let him know?" Johansson asked.

"Sure. No problem. Can I ask why you chose him?" Smith asked.

"I liked his politics," Johansson replied.

The Abduction Scheme
April 24, 2014

The smell of flowers and cooked meat filled the private office. The meat smell wafted in from across the street and the secretary had picked fresh roses, carnations and sunflowers. It was a hot and sweaty day and two worried politicians were meeting about their country's dire situation.

"Over the past three years, they have cost us billions with their abductions, attacks and theft. We just don't have the money or the resources to repel them," the minister of war said to the president.

"I know. We have lost many lives and they have stolen our oil wells and caused us nothing but trouble. We have no help from our neighbors because they are very poor. We have few options," the president explained.

"I have an idea and it's just an idea, so we do," the minister started to say.

"Go ahead. What's your idea? I'm really at the end of my rope. What do you think we should do?" the president asked. He had known the minister for 20 years, so he trusted him and his judgment. They even rode camels and ate together.

"I have some men who haven't been trained in the military very much. They're more like a goat herder militia, I like to call them," the minister started to say.

"Uh huh. Oh, I like this. Please go on," the president said.

"Well, I have about 80 men who can dress like a terror group and steal some children from the girl's school and ask for a ransom. They have a place to house them for up to a month and they also have the transport vehicles. A local mission will supply the food and volunteers, we're sure.

We won't be able to pay and we can appeal to everyone for aid. We can also request emergency aid because the World United Federation could give us about 50 times what they give us now. We badly need it for infrastructure, protection and development," the minister explained.

A concerned look landed on the president's face. His hand rubbed his cheek and then his forehead.

"Okay. Let's do it. I'm willing to take a risk like that. We have nothing. We are in debt and we will never get out of it. Let's take a chance. Let's do it," the president said.

Three days later the goat herder militia stole about 300 children from the local girl's school. They loaded them into giant trucks and drove them 77 miles away in the middle of the night.

"Where are you taking us?" one little girl asked her captor.

"We are taking you on a little vacation, sweetheart. Nobody will hurt you. We're going to have a big meal when you get there and then you can pet some animals. Think of it as a vacation because you will have everything you need and when you go home, we will all have much, much more," the abductor replied.

"Okay. Please don't hurt us. I have to get home to my mommy and daddy," she said.

False Alarm
April 25, 2014

"Someone is at the door, honey. Do you want me to get it?" Hans' wife asked.

"I will. Don't worry about it," Hans said, unlocking and slowly opening the front door.

As he swung the door open, three men in uniform with badges stood in the doorway. He recognized them as local College Park police officers because of the emblem they wore. Behind the officers, a tall man in a navy blue suit and red tie was approaching the door and he walked in between the officers and spoke.

"Hello, sir. We'd like to talk to you. Can we come in for a minute?" Mr. Jackson politely asked.

"Sure. What is this all about?" Hans asked, allowing the four men to enter and sit on the sectional sofa. Hans grabbed a wooden chair from the kitchen table and sat in front of them. His wife stopped cleaning dishes to listen and their son was asleep because he had school the next day.

"How are you guys enjoying the United States?" Mr. Jackson asked. They were immigrants from Germany living in College Park, Maryland for the past two years. Hans looked for work each week, but the family was supported by welfare.

"I've been looking for work. My wife Aubrey works hard at home and volunteers at the hospital. Our son Axel attends third grade at McMillan Elementary School on Concord Street," Hans explained.

At McMillan elementary, there were seven large classes for first grade through sixth grade. With more than 1500 students, McMillan attracted local students and some kids were bused there from surrounding areas. In an area where many of the schools received a lot of funding because of the influential, government-employed families, this school stood out because it didn't get much funding at all, even though it was about 14 miles away from Washington, D.C.

"Hans, we have a gun epidemic in America. I don't know if you've been watching the news or not, but people keep walking into schools and opening fire. Schools don't have sufficient security or funding and it has been happening in Maryland and across the country and it's my job to stop it," Mr. Jackson explained.

"Yes. I've seen the violence on the news and I am very worried for my son's safety. Some kids have threatened him, he said. It seems to be a harsh environment for him and I have thought about pulling him out of the school," Hans said.

"Well, I'm sorry to hear that. It sounds like things have been very difficult for you guys," Mr. Jackson said and paused.

"Yes. In Germany, I taught German language classes at the university and my wife worked as a nurse. Axel attended a private school he loved and things were very good. We came to America hoping they would get even better, but they have not gotten better. They are much worse," Hans said.

"Again, I'm very sorry. Many people come to America and discover it's a struggle to pay the bills and get ahead. Immigrants like you guys are often trained in their home country to do something and come here and cannot find a job in that field.

Listen. I know you're discontent and I have a solution for you. Since we want stricter gun laws to protect school kids, more security funding and we want you guys to be happy, I will make you a deal that will help us and you guys. If you let us stage a fake shooting at your son's school, we will give you guys $600,000 and pay for all of your relocating expenses," Mr. Jackson said.

"A fake shooting? What do you mean by that?" Hans asked.

"Well, this is what we'll do. Next week, we will conduct an active shooter situation at your son's school, but he won't be harmed. The shooter will really be a government agent and your son will be wearing a fake blood vest. He will pretend to shoot your son and he will be rushed to the hospital before another actor shoots the shooter and we take him away. You'll meet your son at the hospital and he will be released to you and you, Aubrey and Axel will need to leave the country immediately."

"I think I understand. When will we get the money?" Hans asked.

"We will pay you one of two ways and you can decide which way you prefer. We want you to be happy and relocate, so we can either pay you by electronic funds transfer or in Goldman Sachs stocks," Mr. Jackson replied.

"I think we'd prefer the cash. Can you give me a minute while I talk this over with my wife?" Hans asked.

"Sure. Go right ahead. I'm going to make a phone call," Mr. Jackson said, pulling out his cell phone and beginning to dial. Hans met Aubrey in the kitchen and they talked in lowered voices.

"What do you think about their offer?" Hans asked.

"I can't believe it. I can't believe they're giving us this opportunity. You know, if we do it, we can't tell anyone," Aubrey said.

"I know. It would have to be our secret. Wow, $600,000 and relocation expenses. That's a lot of money. That's like $200,000 for each of us. Plus, it would probably cost about $5,000 to move everything back home," Hans said.

"Yeah, I know. Let's do it! I don't like it here. It's too hard and I miss home," Aubrey said.

"Okay, but do you think this is a safe plan?" Hans asked.

"I think it's twisted, but I think Axel will be safe and that's all that really matters. He hated that school anyway and if it helps the school and the children, then why not?" Aubrey explained and asked.

Hans paused and thought. This was a dishonest plan, but it wasn't his plan, so he didn't feel guilty about it. He had suspected that the government was dishonest and this confirmed it for him. Hans wondered if they were opportunistic and if the ends justified the means to them, but he didn't have to wonder anymore.

"Yeah. I think it's time for us to get out of here. I've been really concerned about the spying and terrorism and I think this was just the final thing for me. Let's accept their cash offer and move back home," Hans said.

Four days later, at McMillan Elementary School, a man with a gun entered Axel's classroom. It looked like a real gun, but it actually fired a pellet at Axel's chest. Hitting the blood vest, it sprayed fake blood everywhere and looked very real.

Axel's teacher pulled the fire alarm and it wailed while the assistant teacher called the police. The shooter ran down the long hallway, through the cafeteria, past the administration offices and exited the building as the police arrived. One officer who was trained for this shot the shooter with a pellet in his blood vest, pretending to kill him.

The ambulance arrived for Axel and took him to the hospital and another ambulance came soon after and took the shooter away.

Four days later, the family was back home and the money was transferred to their bank account like Mr. Jackson promised. They lived happily ever after and never spoke of the fantastic event.

Extra Supporters
April 25, 2014

"Thanks for meeting me here today. You are appreciated. Please sit down and I will address all of you about the exciting business opportunity," Mr. Yook Sang smiled and said.

250 women were applying to pose as fans for the president. They were essentially like Hollywood extras.

"Thank you for your interest. Let me explain our generous offer to you. You have been selected from hundreds of applicants to attend President Ming's press conference on May 3. We will need you to be there from 8 a.m. until 2 p.m. We will provide lunch and give you $150 for your service," Mr. Sang explained until a hand went up and he recognized it.

"What will we need to wear?" the woman asked.

"Come in loose clothing and we will give you a uniform to wear. We want everyone to look very clean, similar and professional," Mr. Sang said and another hand went up, so he recognized it.

"Will we get to meet the president?" she asked.

"Maybe. Some people might meet him, but we do not know if he will be in a hurry or not or how he will be feeling," Mr. Sang said and continued. "We will conduct a parade and feature some of our military vehicles and weapons, but you won't be too close to them, so don't worry. You will be safe and you will need to cheer when we signal you.

At 2 p.m., you will receive your pay. You'll stand in line at the cashier and get the money for your work. There might be a special opportunity for some of you, so be prepared for another offer. If there aren't any more questions, I need to go and I will see you on May 3!" Mr. Sang said and left.

Two weeks later, it was May 3 and the 250 women came to the jobsite. All of them came on time and Mr. Sang was there, too.

"Thank you for coming, ladies. I have very good news. Our sponsor has agreed to double your pay! You all get $300 each, so make sure you cry, scream and yell for the president! Let's go!" Mr. Sang excitedly said. The women started weeping and walking to the press conference.

Suddenly, the president's car approached and they screamed and yelled, waving and crying. These ladies were poor and $300 was a lot of money for one day's work, so they were extremely excited. It even made them forget about the president's horrible human right's record and the way he considers himself a god.

The First GMO Oil
April 27, 2014

"I don't think anyone is going to like it with all the acid. It makes the oil taste bitter and if people eat too much, it could be toxic," Dr. Rasmussen said to his boss, Johnny O.T. Spot.

"We just have so much of it and it grows quickly and easily. It could be a major competitor in the oil market," Johnny said.

"Well, my scientists have noticed several varieties that have lower acidity. If we bred those ones, we could keep breeding them and using the offspring with the lowest acidity until there is almost none remaining. It might take a few years, though," Dr. Rasmussen said.

"Yes. I like that idea. Let's hope the acid doesn't play an important role in the oil's structure. And we don't have years, but let's go with that idea and evaluate it in three months," Johnny said.

For three months, the scientists worked with the plants and were able to reduce the amount of acid they produced by selecting the ones that made the least acid and crossbreeding those ones. However, they were only able to lower it by 6%.

Johnny set up a meeting with Dr. Rasmussen to discuss his progress.

"We have made some progress. In fact, we were able to reduce the amount of undesirable acidity by 6%. I estimate we can remove about 6% more in six months. The process will take progressively longer as there is less acid, so after six more months, we can evaluate everything and we should have reduced the original acid content by about one eighth," Dr. Rasmussen said.

"I don't think we have that long. Is there anything else you can do?" Johnny asked.

"There really isn't. We have to wait until the plants grow enough to be tested and then we must finish the plants' growing process to maturity and breed them. It takes time," Dr. Rasmussen explained.

"Okay. Well, I've been talking to a guy about genetically modifying the plant and his team has been working on it for a while. It could speed up our work and bring us to harvest and production right away. What do you think?" Johnny asked.

"If the plant was genetically modified, the amount of acid could be reduced or even eliminated if we knew which gene was producing it. However, we would also have to label it GMO and it would be worth less. And we couldn't sell any organic oil that way," Dr. Rasmussen said.

Johnny thought and wondered about the best course of action. On one hand, he wanted to hurry and sell this new oil. Food manufacturers wanted it because it was a cheaper alternative to olive oil, sunflower oil and safflower oil and the auto and manufacturing industries wanted it as a lubricant.

"What if we genetically engineer it, but keep it a secret? How would they know if we used natural selection or genetic engineering?" Johnny asked.

"Well, since the oil has never been used before, we have the exclusive patent on it. If we keep it under our control, I don't think anyone outside this room would ever know. After its genome is changed, nobody will know because nobody has the original plant to compare it to. If other companies want to produce it, they will have to find a way to reduce the acid, but they won't know how we did it," Dr. Rasmussen thoughtfully explained.

Two weeks later, after meeting the other scientists, they choose the genetically modified crop and they eliminated almost all of the acid in a matter of days. They also quickly grew and harvested the plants, produced the oil and sold it on the market, without telling anyone what they did, for a handsome profit.

The Popularity Package
April 28, 2014

"There are so many options! This is exciting," the rock star said.

"Well, take a good look at them and we'll give you a few minutes to decide which one you want," the agent said.

Brita was the singer and guitarist for an up-and-coming rock band called Titans. She wanted to improve her popularity and increase her fan base, so she was listening to her agent's advice and meeting Lydia. Lydia was an agent who specialized in social media exposure at New World Media.

Brita carefully read the colorful brochure. There were five options and they read:

1. $2000 - Domestic tour package (20 US shows)

2. $4000 - International tour package (20 foreign shows)

3. $500 - Promo photo package

4. $2000 - Celebrity photos

5. $500 - Double remarks and reviews

* NWM works with celebrities who give their permission to be photoshoped into a photograph with you, but your fake tour must be in their city. We have deals with several major celebrities in every major city.

* NWM monitored accounts will post positive reviews on Yelp, Trip Adviser, Facebook and Twitter.

* NWM will independently pretend to sell tickets to your fake tour to the public on the Internet and each show will sell out.

* After you give us promo pictures or purchase the promo package, we will Photoshop you into pictures with fans at each venue.

* NWM will post about your concert on Facebook's and Twitter's fake venue pages.

* NWM will use many different fake accounts to post positive messages about each show.

At the bottom of the card it said: "Don't forget you must agree to stay indoors during the time of your fake tour. Plan ahead and you could be at home or preferably somewhere else."

Fit For Radio
April 30, 2014

"And if you're caller number 20, you'll win $1,000. Good luck!" Carson the radio DJ said to the listeners. Immediately, phone calls flooded the station.

"The phones are lighting up!" Bobby the assistant said. Within a few minutes, 19 people had called.

"All right. The next caller is number 20!" Bobby said. Like the other calls, they let their answering machine answer the call and put them on hold while they searched for information by their phone number.

"Let's see what we've got. Sherman Samuels is 55 years old. He rents a house in Bell and he's a registered Republican. He drives a 2009 Chevy truck and works for Bob's Straw Hut. Last year, he went on vacation to Thailand and he voted for Mitt Romney. Hmmm. I don't think so," Bobby said. Sherman was obviously conservative and this was a very liberal radio station.

"Isn't there any more info?" Carson asked.

"Oh yeah. This software tells me everything except for what he ate for dinner last night and it might just know that, too," Bobby said.

"Let's take a look at number 21," Carson said.

"Number 21 is a blocked caller, so we have no info," Bobby said.

"How about caller 22?" Carson asked.

"Caller number 22 is Pam Ryker. She is a single mother and a Democrat. She rents an apartment in Torrance and drives a 2010 Nissan Pathfinder. Pam has worked as a stripper at Déjà Vu Showgirls for four years. Do you wanna give her the $1,000?" Bobby asked.

"Sure. Sounds good," Carson replied.

The Overserved Scheme
May 18, 2014

"So, are you sure 20% is okay with you?" John asked Dr. Tokowitz.

"Yeah, that's fine. Just come to my office after the accident and I'll give you an exam. I'll print your diagnosis, give you a hard copy and I'll submit it to your insurance company, so they can cover your medical expenses," Dr. Tokowitz said.

"Thanks, doc. I really appreciate it," John said. He and Dr. Tokowitz had been friends for 40 years. They met on the playground in Harlem, New York when they were just 10 years old. After going to elementary school and high school together, John played semi-professional baseball for two years, but he never made it to the major leagues because he hurt his ankle sliding into home.

After high school, Dr. Tokowitz attended New York University and Harvard Medical School. He was an intern and an assistant for a few years before becoming a successful hospital doctor. Eventually, he opened his own office and started a private practice.

"I can't believe I'm gonna do this. I have so many bills. I might get evicted. I just want to fix everything and get my life back on track," John explained and rubbed his forehead with his palms.

"Just be careful. I'll help you any way I can. You're like a brother to me. Okay?" Dr. Tokowitz asked and put a hand on John's shoulder. Over the years, they had kept in touch by phone and email. Several times a year, they went to a baseball game, restaurant, concert, movie or bar to catch up. Since Dr. Tokowitz was an only child, he felt like John was like a brother to him.

"I'm gonna crash into a corner house at 30 miles an hour, but I'll wear my seatbelt, so I should be fine. You can tell me for sure at my exam!" John said and laughed, seemingly unbothered about the potential for injury or even death.

John was plotting to collect insurance money after pretending to be badly injured. He was also going to sue the Open Bar for overserving him, which he'll say led to him crashing his car. John hoped to make hundreds of thousands of dollars in the lawsuit and get a new car, even if it meant getting a little bruised or injured. His bills and debts stressed him, so John felt like he was at the end of his rope and had no other options. The money was going to help him pay off his credit cards and get back on his feet.

The next night, John drove to the Open Bar and ordered pints of dark beer and vodka shots. It was a very busy night because it was Lady's Night and drinks were half off. He held his alcohol very well and he didn't talk or move much except to walk to the bathroom to urinate, so they served him six pints and six shots in less than three hours.

After one last bathroom trip, John walked to his truck and opened the door. Getting in, he could barely see straight and everything was blurry. Turning the key and starting the engine, he fastened his seatbelt and drove as carefully as possible. Unfortunately, he still weaved a little and he couldn't stay in between the lines very well. It was so late, there wasn't any other traffic on the road.

Luckily, the road to the house he wanted to hit was straight and simple. However, he accidentally picked up extra speed and hit it driving 50 miles an hour, destroying the corner of the home and scattering broken glass everywhere. The occupants were not home, so nobody immediately rushed to see what happened.

The impact threw John through the windshield and on the ground. Miraculously, he wasn't injured very badly.

The neighbors called the police and about 10 minutes later, they arrived and arrested John for driving under the influence of alcohol. At the police station, he blew a 1.8 in the blood alcohol breath machine, which meant he was very drunk and over twice the state's legal limit. In fact, they marveled at the way John wasn't seriously ill, badly injured or dead.

After John was arraigned and left jail, he took a taxi to Dr. Tokowitz's office for his exam and diagnosis.

"Ouch, ouch," John said as Dr. Tokowitz applied pressure to his shoulder.

"Turn your head right," the doctor said. When John did, he moaned in pain and wasn't able to turn it very far.

"Now to the left," Dr. Tokowitz said and John obeyed. Grimacing in pain, he wasn't able to turn very much in that direction either.

"I need to x-ray your collarbone and part of your spine. You might have a fractured or broken collarbone or spine," Dr. Tokowitz said.

For the next 20 minutes, Dr. Tokowitz and his assistant x-rayed John and developed the pictures. After the assistant scanned the x-rays into the computer, the doctor closely examined them.

"You have a complex fracture in your right collarbone," Dr. Tokowitz said, pointing to a spot on his collarbone with a ballpoint pen. "Your left one is only bruised. It'll take several weeks of rest for your right side to heal and I need to immobilize it, so it doesn't get any worse."

"Okay. Just document everything. I'm going to sue the crap out of these guys," John said, gingerly moving his head back and forth.

"No problem. Is that sufficient or would you like me to make up a broken arm or something?" Dr. Tokowitz half-jokingly asked.

"Yeah, that would be great. Any believable injury that costs about $10,000 to fix would be awesome. Could you also write in the notes how you think I was overserved at the bar and that was the reason this happened?" John asked.

"Sure. And if you need me to be a witness in court, just let me know," Dr. Tokowitz said.

"Great. I'll let you know after we get our court date and I talk to my attorney," John said.

Dr. Tokowitz submitted the information to John's insurance company and they paid the bill to fix his collarbone. They also paid $8,950 to fix his arm, which they split 80/20.

A few weeks later, John sued the Open Bar in civil court for overserving him. During an early phase of the trial, before the jury reached a verdict, the bar's attorney settled with John and wrote him a check for $200,000. After John paid the city of Sacramento $2,400 for the DUI and his attorney $3,000 for his fees, he kept $194,600, so he was able to pay off his debts, buy a new car and save some money, albeit dishonestly.

Worried Hate Assessment
May 26, 2004

Prince Abdullah sat at his cedar desk with a calculator in one hand and some bills on the other one. Punching in number after number, he began to sweat. His country needed to pay several bills or the companies were going to charge them late fees.

At that moment, his aide slowly opened the office door and politely asked if he was busy. Abdullah said no and invited him to sit on the sofa and speak to him.

"Did the transfer come yet?" Muhammad asked. He was referring to $120 million in aid money his country was supposed to get.

"Not yet. It was supposed to be here yesterday and we have bills to pay," Abdullah worriedly said.

"Did you try calling them?" Muhammad asked.

"Yeah, I thought about it. I just feel funny." Abdullah unlocked his iPhone to check his email, but he got distracted with a game he just downloaded called Kwazy Kaliphs.

"Well, what are we going to do? Who won't get paid? Will they shut off the electricity, again?"

"I just don't understand why they haven't sent it, yet," he said without answering. "Do you think they're going to send it this month?" Abdullah asked. Even though Abdullah hired Muhammad and was older and wiser, he still liked to bounce questions off Muhammad. He was a good listener and knew a lot.

"Probably. Why wouldn't they? Do you think they heard about the 'Death to America!' chants at prayer time?" Muhammad shrugged and asked with his palms open.

"No. I don't think so. Maybe their bank has a problem. Maybe it's run by Jews!"

"Calm down. It went through last month. Did you count the number of days?" Muhammad inquired.

"Yes. It's two days longer. EFTs automatically go right through every 30 days. If it didn't go through then, I don't know if it ever will. This is Wednesday and it should have been here Monday," Abdullah explained.

"Do you think they heard about the way we burned their flags last week?"

"Were they in the news? I thought we told the media they couldn't report about them," Abdullah said.

"Right, right. We did, but maybe there are independent journalists or more Al Jazeera reporters who are telling them about things."

"That's possible. Maybe I should call them today or tomorrow," Abdullah said and longingly looked out the window.

$120 million was a lot of money to them and their country. Their economy wasn't that big and it was struggling. They hated feeling like the transferred money might not come and they also hated feeling like they were walking on eggshells. They knew how much the people hated America, yet they had to perform a balancing act, like walking on a tightrope each month to continue getting the money.

The two men decided to get lunch down the street and wait to see if the EFT came in the afternoon. They returned to the office 90 minutes later and the phone rang. It was Colonel Mustard calling on behalf of General Anesthetic and Major Mott.

"Hi! Colonel Mustard! How are you doing, sir?" Abdullah respectfully asked.

"I'm well. Call me Michael. I'm on vacation in the Poconos. I just wanted to let you know the EFT will go through tomorrow. There was a slight delay, but don't worry. It'll be there. Okay?"

"Great! Fantastic. Thanks and good to hear. Please have a safe vacation and return trip home, sir," Abdullah said, showing his appreciation.

"You bet. And you guys try to keep the flag burning to a minimum, all right?"

"Yes sir!"

The next day, the money was there.

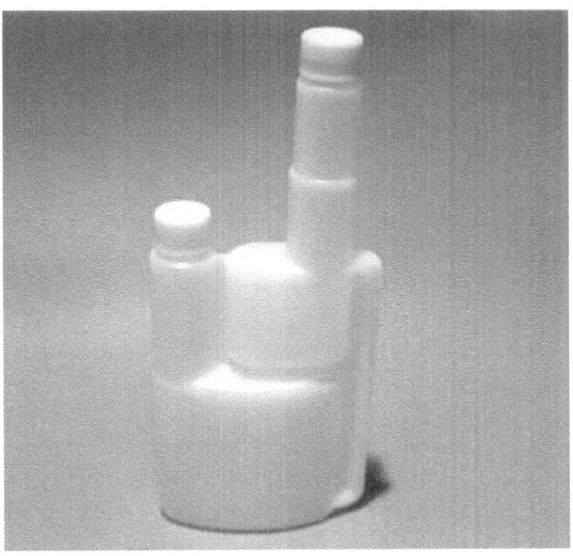

The Additive Weapon
July 12, 2014

On a sunny afternoon in a musty bomb shelter, Ahmed was proud of his new invention. Holding up a small, white plastic bottle that looked like octane booster, he proudly explained what was in it to Muhammad.

"I've been experimenting with deadly chemicals for months and I've finally found the right mixture." Ahmed was a chemist at the local university and he routinely taught and experimented.

"What should we do with it?" Muhammad asked.

"All we have to do is pour it in a car's fuel tank and it'll poison whoever breathes the exhaust. I've been experimenting without testing it in a car and I think a 10 to 1 ratio of gasoline to poison will be perfect."

"Perfect for what? What's the plan and who do you want to test it on?"

"I don't know, but it's better than a typical bomb because it's invisible. Nobody will suspect anything and by the time they feel sick, we'll already be gone."

"Let's test it on the Christians at the church down the street and if it works, we can use it on the Zionists," Muhammad said. Ahmed smiled from ear to ear and nodded his head.

Neither of them liked Christians or Jews because they felt marginalized and oppressed by them. In reality, some of their ancestors and their radical Muslim friends were partly to blame for their current situation. Many of them lived in poverty and some were jailed for crimes they didn't commit. Some of their innocent friends and family members had even been killed by accident because of their affiliations.

"Great idea! On Sunday we will test it on the churchgoers and see if they get sick or die and then we'll know if we should change the potency before we poison the Zionists."

"I'll be here. Will we use your car?"

"Yes. Be here at 7 a.m. and we'll test our new weapon!" Ahmed exclaimed. Muhammad agreed and they parted ways.

Three days later, it was Sunday and Muhammad came over on time. When he arrived, Ahmed was pouring the poison into his gas tank. He had already filled the tank with 10 gallons of gas. Five minutes later, they were driving to the nearby church.

The First Baptist Church of Bethraza held about 1,000 people and their 7:30 a.m. service was the most popular one and about 900 people usually attended. Attendees typically arrived around 7 a.m. to socialize and drink strong coffee before the church service. Since a long line wrapped around the building, they were an easy target for Ahmed's Ford Festiva's additive weapon.

"I'll drive very slowly by the line of people. When I stop toward the front, I want you to get out and pretend the front license plate is loose. Don't smoke and don't breathe deeply and it'll give the exhaust some extra time to permeate the atmosphere," Ahmed said, driving slowly and carefully. Muhammad nodded and when Ahmed stopped the car, he jumped out and walked to the front. Acting like the license plate was loose,

Muhammad used his fingers to tighten the four screws. After a few minutes, he reentered the car and they slowly drove away.

The next day Muhammad bought a newspaper on the way to Ahmed's house. Reading the front page, he was excited and nervous. He could hardly believe what he saw.

Below a picture of numerous dead bodies lying on the ground, the caption read, "Noxious chemicals were ingested by hundreds of Christians waiting in line for church, sickening 420 people and killing 72 churchgoers."

Just In Case
July 18, 2014

"Put him through," the president said to his aide. Dennis Kastrow hadn't heard from his old friend Vladimir Zurin for a few weeks, but he was always eager to talk to him. They were kindred spirits and powerful leaders even though their people were from entirely different parts of the world.

"Dennis? Vlad here. Watcha doin?"

"Vladimir! What are you doing? We just smoked some cigars and shot six people with a firing squad! Execution style. Women were wailing and it was quite a scene. How about you?" Dennis asked.

"I'm fine. I want to talk business for a minute. I can talk on the phone, but I want to see you, too," Vlad explained.

"No problem. This isn't about the poker game, is it? I won that game fair and square. I don't care what the hooker or the midget say!" Dennis exclaimed.

"No. It's about the loan. We can't forgive all of it, but I have good news, old friend. We can forget about most of it, if you do us a favor or two," Vlad said.

Decades ago, Dennis' father led the country and borrowed a lot of money from Vladimir. He thought he could repay it, but after he made some bad investments and his country suffered setbacks from storms, cartels, looting, and rioting, they sank deeper and deeper into debt. Now Dennis' country owed almost $40 billion, so this was amazing news to him.

"You're joking. Right? Tell me you're joking. That's amazing! Thank you. We'll give you anything. Just name it!" Dennis exclaimed.

"I'll be there in three days and I'll tell you when I see you," Vladimir said and hung up the phone. Three days later, his private jet landed in Savannah and Dennis was waiting for him.

A black, private car drove the two men and their bodyguards to an underground meeting room. Since the island wasn't that big, they built a lot of things underground. It helped them maximize their space and it was more private.

The driver knew the secret key code to get the car into the underground lot, but nobody else even knew the location. However, Dennis and Vlad had met there twice before.

After they exited the vehicle and entered the meeting room, Dennis pulled a small, wooden box out of his desk. Opening it, the smell of tobacco filled the room. He didn't even have to say anything before they grabbed a cigar and started smoking.

"I wish I could stay longer. I just have to deal with a few issues back home," Vlad said.

"I totally understand. If we built that infrastructure and lost it all without any compensation, we'd defend it too, no matter what anyone said," Dennis related. He was referring to a sort of civil war Vlad's country had recently been dragged into because of prior investments underneath land that later became independent.

"Listen. We are happy to forgive your debt. With all due respect, we don't think you would ever be able to repay it. In return, we want to reopen the spy base in the south."

"Consider it done. Will it be just like last time or will you build more installations?" Dennis asked.

"We will build above ground and underground. We will also ship submarine, helicopter, and airplane parts to the island and build them. We will monitor the capitalists and watch as they slowly lose their senseless grip on the world," Vlad said.

"Mi casa es su casa!" Dennis replied; which was an old Spanish phrase meaning, "my house is your house."

"We just can't give you the land. Stay here as long as you want. We'll draw up a contract and I'll give it to the government and it'll be your lease."

"That's too bad. I was hoping we could annex the south and make it part of my federation!" Vlad jokingly said and they laughed hysterically and embraced.

Pulling some vodka from a liquor cabinet, each grizzled man grabbed a shot glass. After Dennis poured them each a 2-ounce shot of top shelf vodka, he said, "To our new union and to the new world!"

"Yes and to US!" Vlad said and they clanked their glasses together and tossed the rancid liquid down the hatch.

Rubber Valley
July 20, 2014

This year's mayoral race was still too close to call. Since they started letting people vote online, more than 90% of Rubber Valley's population voted. In fact, they even let people vote before Election Day.

The incumbent, Richard Rasmussen was running against an unknown challenger named Ricardo Sanchez. In Rubber Valley, Roger district and Bush district had already finished voting and they were only waiting on the Carl district to finish. Since Carl was situated on the west side of town, it was actually in another time zone, so those residents had an extra hour to vote.

Maria volunteered to help the Carl district voters vote. She monitored 30 computers that people used to vote in the community center. It was also her job to watch the vote tally online.

As Maria looked at her laptop, her webcam and microphone were on, but she didn't know it. Several miles away, a hacker was watching her. He had already hacked the voting software and even though Rasmussen was 32 votes ahead, it wouldn't matter soon.

When the hacker heard Maria say she was going to use the bathroom, he added 45 votes to Sanchez's total. Maria didn't see the votes change and she didn't suspect anything after she returned.

After the final hour of voting ended, the votes were counted and Sanchez won by 3 votes and became the next mayor of Rubber Valley.

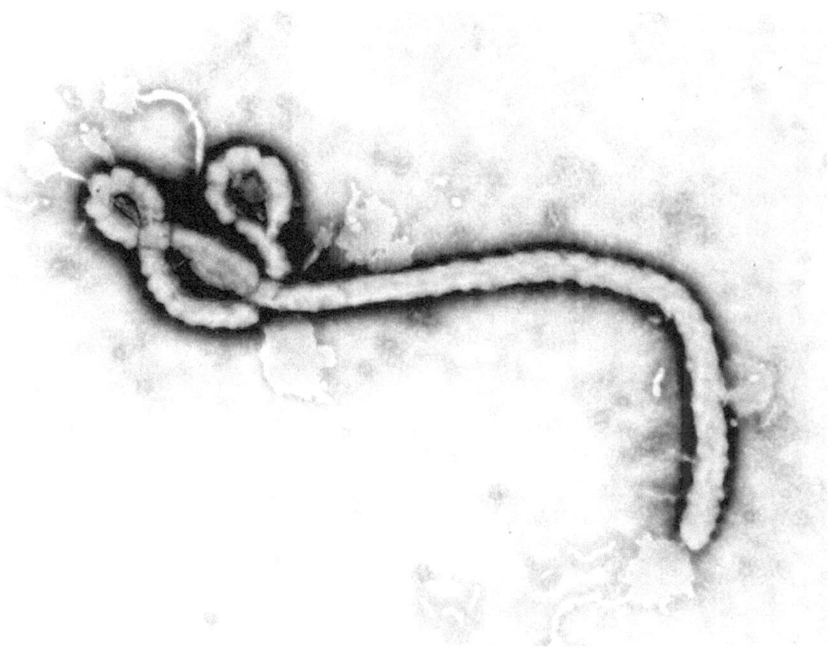

The Fever (Part 1)
July 29, 2014

"This thing is legendary. It's almost like it can jump from person to person!" Dr. Paul Wilson said to his colleague Dr. Jim Brown on the phone. Dr. Wilson had been working in Africa and fighting a deadly, contagious disease. It infected its host and turned them into a bloody mess.

"How many people have been infected?" Dr. Brown asked.

"Well, let's see. I got here after 12 people were diagnosed with 'the fever' and they all died. Since then, we've diagnosed 3,211 people and we've been treating them," Dr. Wilson explained.

"That's certainly one epidemic you have on your hands. How many people have died so far?" Dr. Brown asked.

"2,782 have died here. We're hopeful that the rest who are receiving treatment will pull through, but some of them could die too."

"I'm sorry to hear it. Well, they have the right guy on the job with you there," Dr. Brown said.

"Listen. I want to cure this disease. I'm sick of seeing people dying and it's spreading. It used to be found only deep in the jungle, but now it's in the city. If we're not extremely careful and lucky, 'the fever' is going to infect the masses."

"I hope you can cure it. We have your back. You know everyone here is pulling for you and we will do everything we can," Dr. Brown said. In North Carolina, the doctors worked together and studied diseases. They had been researching this one for many years and both of them had worked in the field against different outbreaks.

"I want to bring back two villagers, so we can study them and find a cure. I want to bring a male and a female who are infected and in the early onset stage. If we can isolate the antibodies their immune system is making, we might be able to create a cure or even a vaccine."

"You're probably right, but we can't just fly two African villagers to the United States as guinea pigs. I'd be surprised if they'd agree, but even if they did, there would probably be an international outcry against it. And would we pay them for their time? How would we even communicate with them?" Dr. Brown asked.

These were very good questions that Dr. Wilson hadn't considered. He had been tirelessly working 12-hour days in the field and he hadn't had much time to develop his plan. Each day, it took him 1-2 hours just to take his protective clothing on and off and change it several times. He had lost 15 pounds, but half of it was water weight.

"You brought up some great points. Let me think about it and I'll get back to you. I gotta go," Dr. Wilson said and hung up the phone.

Later that evening, he thought of a better way. If he were to become infected with 'the fever', then they would immediately fly him back to North Carolina, so he could be treated by Dr. Brown's medical team. He knew it was a serious risk, but he thought it was worth it. What if this disease infected millions of people? He had the opportunity to possibly heal people and save an untold number of lives.

The next day, while he was treating one of the patients, he took off one of his gloves. This patient was particularly bloody and within a few seconds, his blood was all over the doctor's hand. That was all it took to get infected.

Later that afternoon, another doctor who was treating patients also came down with 'the fever'. Nobody knew how she contracted it, but she flew back to the US with Dr. Brown.

TO BE CONTINUED

Crack
July 31, 2014

On a warm summer day in a quiet office in Washington, D.C., two politicians who usually opposed each other were discussing a controversial bill.

"It just isn't that bad," Senator Rand Paul said to Senator Harry Reid.

"Okay. If you say so. Haha. We weren't willing to vote for your bill to put 1,000 windmills on every Indian reservation, but we will vote for this," Senator Reid said.

"That's great. I can't thank you enough. Let me know when you guys need a close vote and I've got your back, Senator," Paul said.

"No problem. Will do. Now, you're sure this is wise?"

"Absolutely. The United States will save $1.4 billion in 10 years when possessing small amounts of crack cocaine is only an infraction. Fewer people will be forced through the prison system too. It's really a no brainer."

"Marion Barry seemed to think so!" Reid said and they laughed.

"True that, homie. True that," the independent Kentucky native chimed.

"Oh, I'm also sorry we weren't able to vote for pseudoephedrine decriminalization or the anti-pollution bill. Nobody has ever seen a pseudoephedrine plant and we're all really close to oil and coal companies, so no can do my friend," Reid sympathized.

"I know. I get it. You guys do what ya gotta do and we'll just take it one thing at a time.

Do you think this is the best timing for my bill?"

"Sure. Why not?"

"Well, with everything happening here and abroad, do you think we'll be criticized for not addressing other issues instead right now?" Paul asked.

"I think it's as good of a time as any. We're going on vacation for a month after work tomorrow, so we better vote on it or else we won't vote until mid-September," Reid explained.

"Okay, well I," Paul said and Reid interrupted.

"And don't forget we're also gonna vote on the organic yogurt for youths bill and the international airfare tax. I've gotta go. I'll see you tomorrow," Reid said and he left.

The next day the United States Senate voted 96-3-1 and possessing small amounts of crack cocaine became an infraction. The organic yogurt for youths bill and the international airfare tax decidedly passed as well.

Pull Out and Invest
August 10, 2014

"Haven't we played with their economy enough?" the minister of war jokingly asked the president.

"No. We haven't. If they want to rob us and our friends and hurt our countrymen, then all bets are off. I will do whatever I want, whenever I want, to ensure our assets are protected," the former KGB member said.

"Okay. What would you like us to do now? We already assembled 20,000 soldiers on the southern border."

"I want you to pull them back."

"Pull them back? Like retreat?"

"I didn't say retreat. At 3:30 p.m., I want you to announce we are pulling the armed forces back. Let the commanders know and begin the pull back at 4:30 p.m. Do you understand me?"

"Yes, sir. Is there anything else?"

"That's it for now. I'll be in touch," the socialist leader said and hung up the phone.

His next call was to his finance minister.

"Hello, sir? How can I help you today?" he asked.

"What's the quickest way to make $5 million dollars?"

"I'm sorry, but I don't think I understand the question. Do you need a loan, sir?"

"No. If you needed $5 million tomorrow, what would you do?"

A hush fell over the conversation and after a pregnant pause, the finance minister replied.

"I don't know."

"I want you to cash out $40 million in investment stocks from NIKKEI and invest the funds elsewhere," he said.

"Yes, sir. I can do that. Where should we invest instead?"

"Buy $40 million in stocks from Callon Petroleum," the leader instructed.

"Dow Jones? Okay. Consider it done."

"Listen. I want you to buy them Friday when the market opens at 5:30 p.m. I'll talk to you later. Bye."

"Consider it done."

Later that day, the minister of war made the announcement to the press and began pulling the troops back. An hour later, the finance minister sold $40 million in stocks from the NIKKEI market and bought Callon Petroleum stocks with it. By the end of the day, the stocks had increased in value by 12.5% and they made $5 million dollars.

The Girl With Binoculars
August 12, 2014

As Sheila looked through her binoculars, she could see the wooden park bench by the lake where people often sat to feed the ducks and relax. It was sunny and cool outside and a tall, dark, and handsome man sat down.

"Wow. He's cute," she whispered.

Putting on some pants and a shirt, she looked in the mirror and smiled. She was hot and confident, so she grabbed her book and left.

Her apartment was situated about 100 yards from the lake. It was manmade, but she liked it because of the grass, colorful ducks, and peaceful atmosphere.

Gingerly walking with her gardening book, she looked in Mark's big blue eyes.

"Do you mind if I join you?"

"Sure," he said, scooting over to make room for her on the bench.

They sat a few inches from each other and read. Sheila was reading Growing Great Cannabis and Mark was reading the Dungeon Master's Guide.

It was beautiful outside. The silence was only interrupted by quacking and the wind. After a few minutes, they couldn't be any more relaxed.

A few people were walking around the lake on each side. One of them was walking a big, brown dog on a leash.

"Do you have any pets?" Sheila blurted out. While she looked calm, cool, and collected on the outside, she was actually quite nervous. She knew if she just went for it, she would at least get a response. She only sounded tense because it was so peaceful.

Mark slowly looked up from his book.

"I have a hamster named Sam."

Sheila smiled.

"I love hamsters! I have one too. His name is Rick. Wanna see him?" she smiled and asked, tilting her head to one side and batting her eyes.

"Okay," Mark said. He was the type of guy who was open to suggestion and he didn't have a lot planned at the moment. He didn't mind going on a little adventure into unknown territory. He was also strong and quick and she was quite charming.

"I live right over here. It's really close," she said, taking him by the hand. She really had his attention now.

"You must love it," Mark said.

"I do! It's the best. The rent isn't bad too," she said.

Once they got inside, she motioned for Mark to sit on the sofa and he did.

"Would you like anything to drink?" she asked.

"Some water will be great," he said.

"No vodka?" she joked and they laughed. It was the middle of the day and they just met, so it would be unusual for them to start drinking vodka. It wouldn't be unheard of though and she wanted to be a good hostess.

Sheila walked into the kitchen and poured a cup of water for each of them. Mark took in his surroundings. She was very neat and had some interesting things. A big blue lava lamp was flowing and a big, freshwater fish tank boasted all sorts of fish and crabs.

"Listen, I have a confession to make. I brought you here for a reason," she said.

That got Mark's attention. He sat up and looked at her.

"I'm not a virgin. If this is a virgin sacrifice, I'm sorry. You've got the wrong guy," he joked and they both laughed.

"I want to be a singer and I want you to be brutally honest with me. Can I sing you a few things?" she nervously asked.

"Sure! I'd love to hear you sing. Are they originals or covers?"

"I sing both. I just wanna sing all the time. It's really my passion," she said and shrugged her shoulders, still a little embarrassed. While Sheila felt singing was her calling in life, she wasn't sure when, where, or how she would use her talent.

Suddenly a bomb came through the roof and exploded, instantly killing both of them. Their bloody bodies flew across the room and hit the wall. Mark instinctually put his hand out, so there was a bloody handprint when the coroner came hours later.

Some say it was their fault, but I don't think so. They were born and raised there and it wasn't their fault that they lived in Palestine and Israel lived next door.

The Guber Meeting
August 13, 2014

The air was damp and moist in the downstairs meeting room. It resembled a basement and pictures of old men in hats lined the walls because it was also a Masonic temple.

Once a month, the Guber company met their employees and discussed business in the temple. The ones who couldn't make it watched live via webcam streaming online at a password protected website.

"I'd like to bring this meeting to order. We have several things to discuss and something very exciting that I think you will all like," the president said.

Everyone quieted down. The men and women at the buffet quickly grabbed some chicken and rice along with a drink and returned to their seats. They always asked for an open bar, but they never got one.

"We've been listening to your concerns and we have something I think you're going to like. It's a secret, so you can't tell anyone about it. You'll find a waiver on your table. Please sign it and I'll let Squiggy tell you all about it. Please give him a warm hand," the president said and everyone clapped and signed a waiver.

Squiggy was their tech guy. Many people knew him personally because they've needed help with the online reservation system. It usually worked well, but once in a while it would crash or employees would have a question about something. Squiggy was always quick to answer and fix every problem. He was professional, expeditious, and well-liked.

"Hey you guys. Everybody take out your cell phone real quick. Does everyone have either an iPhone or an Android OS-enabled phone?" Virtually everyone nodded or held up their phone.

"In a minute, I'm going to give you a url for a special application that only you will have. It's called Gubertown. Everybody ready?" Squiggy asked.

"Yeah. What does it do?" one of the employees barked.

"You know those complaints you've been filing?" Squiggy asked.

"Complaints? Like people smelling funny?"

"No. Like people peeing in the back seat!" Ahmed said and the place erupted with laughter.

"Yes. That sort of thing. Well," Squiggy started and was interrupted.

"I had someone with three dogs want a ride for a mile and a half and they didn't even tip me!" Sancho said and a grown fell over the place.

"One time, I had to drive a stinky homeless man to a shelter and I think he left lice in my car!" David Chong chimed and the employees groaned and mumbled.

"Yes, yes. All of those things are legitimate complaints. Here is what we've done. You now have your own application to report these sorts of things! After you leave your passenger at his or her destination, open the app. and rate the passenger. You'll answer a few questions and every driver will have special access to the database to see if they want to pick this passenger up in the future or not."

Everyone was very pleased and started discriminating immediately.

Cuckoo Ka Choo
August 17, 2014

"Totally!" Amy said. She was disgusted.

"And did you see the way she looked at Mark and flirted with him? Someone should tell is wife. He's been married for like eight years and she almost had her top off in his lap!" Arthur her gay black friend said. He recently married his partner. Amy was sort of a former fag hag, but that's another story.

Earlier that day they were filming a television show in Hollywood. When they finished, since it was the end of the week, they celebrated with beer, wine, and alcohol along with some live music by Slash and Steven Tyler. They just happened to stop by.

"Yeah, for sure. Something bad is going to happen to her one of these days. That's just karma," Amy exclaimed, grabbed a two-ounce shot of top shelf tequila, licked some salt, and slammed it, followed by squirting some lime into her mouth.

"It could happen sooner than later. Wanna do it to her? I've hated her ever since she first walked on the set. Did you know she stole Andy's wallet? That's what Joe said. Now she's in line for some sort of promotion, according to Larry," Arthur said, shaking his head. Things get around and they had been working together for a few months.

"Are you serious? How? You're crazy. If we get caught, we'll go to jail forever!" Amy said and looked at Arthur.

"Haha. A few years maybe, but we won't get caught. We won't even be there. I know a guy who works on the set and I can get him to do it. He was just telling me how he'd do it," Arthur said.

"Really? Wow. Okay. Yeah. Let's do it! She's a bitch. Fuck her," Amy gave in. She was insecure and didn't like any competition in her very competitive acting field. Amy's father was a powerful politician in a big city, so she was used to tough talk like that.

Three days ago, Arthur had a very weird conversation with one of the stage hands named Barney. Barney was from a poor Midwestern city and not very educated. Sadly, someone who looked just like the cuckoo starlet Amy and Arthur wanted to kill beat him up when he was a kid. Consequently, he carried a grudge with him toward people who looked like her. She was white, thin, and short with a very large, curved nose and long brown hair.

When Barney saw this woman, he began thinking of ways he could kill her and get away with it. At first, he considered hitting her in the head with a lead pipe. That could knock her senseless or even kill her, but it would get blood everywhere. He'd have to clean it up and it wouldn't be easy.

Barney considered standing above her with a noose and dropping it over her head from above. He could choke her out that way, but then he'd have to run away. Barney wasn't very fast, so he dismissed this idea. He also wanted to keep his job and remain anonymous.

Finally, Barney remembered they were filming with a real train on a train track on Monday. The entire team was doing it in the studio next door. Barney said he could sneak into the area on Sunday and tamper with it, so it would crush her.

Arthur called Barney and told him to do it. It was like music to Barney's ears. He smiled and started obsessively thinking about it.

The next day, Barney snuck into the train room and loosened the brake pedal. It was so loose that when someone tried to break with it a few times, it would eventually fall off. Nobody saw him and he made it in and out very quickly.

On Monday, everyone was in place to film the train scene for a sixth time. The first five times went well, but something small went wrong each time. They all hoped this would be the last take; especially Barney.

"I can't believe you fools got it wrong again. Where's my water?!" the cuckoo starlet yelled. Everyone looked at each other and a few seconds later an agitated intern from the local drama school ran up to her with an opened container of bottled water.

"I don't want this! It's been opened!"

"It's yours. You drank some earlier," the intern said to the starlet.

"I don't care. Get me another one," she said and the intern returned with an unopened bottle about three minutes later.

"It took long enough. When is this thing over? I have stuff to do and these people are idiots," she said. In reality, the people were working hard and doing their job and she was just being a bitch.

"Listen, everyone. Let's make this a good one. It'll be the final take for the day and then we'll all get outta here. Okay?" the producer said. The group sighed in relief and prepared to nail it.

It was a silent scene because the starlet didn't feel like writing any words. She touted herself as a brilliant writer and she was friends with the creator of the show, so when she told him she had a great script, he met her. He had no idea it would be silent. He wanted to give her writing a try and not her weird acting. Nonetheless, she pitched it to him and he caved in to her pressure and said okay against his better judgment.

As the cuckoo starlet and several other girls who she chose because they were fatter and slower than her ran uphill behind the moving train. As it neared the top, the driver pressed the break pedal to the floor and it fell off and quickly rolled backwards toward the ladies. It happened so fast that it ran the starlet over. The train's rear right wheel severed her left leg by the hip. Next, the rear part of the train hit her torso and she did an aerial backflip. After she landed on her back, the train ran over her left arm, severing it at the shoulder. Within a minute, she bled out and died.

Barney, Amy, Arthur, and others restrained their jubilation, but they were very pleased with the outcome. Nobody was ever charged with a crime and it was ruled an accidental death.

A Bear With Benefits
August 18, 2014

<u>Note</u>: This story contains adult themes.

"Dude, I'm all over it! Just let me take a quick shower and I'll watch it with you. K?" Maurice said to Ronnie.

"You always say that, man. The Cavs are playing the Heat for the first time since LeBron returned to Cleveland. I thought you'd wanna watch it with me," Ronnie said. They liked basketball a lot. Maurice was busy and he rarely had time for his roommate Ronnie, but he liked him and tried to spend time with him. Maurice had nothing else to do tonight, so he sincerely wanted to watch the basketball game.

"No. I'll be ready. Is the tip off at six?"

"Yeah."

"I'll be outta the shower in 10 minutes," Maurice said, grabbing his phone and running into the bedroom. He was a people-pleaser, which was tough because he spread himself thin between work, family, and friendly obligations. After he took off his shirt, he got a text. It was Gina.

"I want your ding dong!" she exclaimed. Although Maurice was gay, they frequently fooled around with each other. Gina loved cunnilingus and he gave it to her whenever she wanted. In return, he sometimes got a blow job, but she typically gave him a hand job, or a combination of the two sex acts. She told everyone she had TMJ, so she wouldn't ever have to give blow jobs, but she was lying.

"I bet you do, but I have to watch a basketball game with Ron," he replied.

"Seriously? I had a horrible day at work and I really need you to wrap your big luscious lips around my vagina," she wrote. She was a prideful, demanding, Hollywood actress and frequently had run-ins with people she felt she was better than. She wasn't much, but her dad was an attorney and her brother was a business man and she felt tough because of their power and success. Her parents divorced when she was very little and that was part of the reason why she had issues. Maurice was a little afraid of her because she blew up from time to time, but never when she wanted sex. She was really nice then.

Maurice was conflicted. On one hand, he wanted to please his roommate. On the other hand, he wanted to please Gina and himself. After thinking for a minute, he texted her back.

"Okay. Come asap."

"Great! See u soon!" she replied.

Maurice returned to the living room and spoke to Ronnie.

"Listen. Something came up. I gotta talk to Gina, man. Raincheck on the game?"

"I knew you'd flake. What does she want now? That chick's a crazy slut, homie." Ronnie was right.

"Be that as it may, she had a really bad day and she needs me. Okay?" Maurice asked.

"Fine."

Maurice took a quick shower and when he got out, Gina was already sitting on his bed in her bra and panties. She had her own key, but Ronnie would have let her in anyway.

"Are you ready to eat my cunt?" she asked, spreading her legs and tilting her head.

"Bring those pussy lips over here!" he said in a deep voice. She pulled off her underwear and crawled to his side of the bed and laid on her back. Maurice gave her cunnilingus for an hour and he stopped when his jaw started hurting a lot.

"That was just what I needed. Now bring that beautiful dick over here," Gina said. Maurice removed his underwear and he sat beside her with a partly erect penis. She put her mouth on it and sucked his dick for about two minutes and he became hard. Taking it out of her mouth, she continued with her hand.

"I'm about to come. Hang on," he said. To distract himself, Maurice liked to turn on AM news radio. He quickly turned the station to 1070 AM and spread his legs for her again. She continued rubbing up and down.

"We have some breaking news. Bill Cosby was found dead in his house this morning with a fatal gunshot wound to the head. The police haven't released the details yet, but when they do, we will bring it to you live," the radio broadcaster said.

Instantly, Maurice's penis became soft. This wasn't just the gentle distraction he wanted. Cosby was his childhood idol, so he was devastated.

"Oh my God. Did you hear that? Bill Cosby is dead. I can't do this now. I'm not in the mood. Thanks though," Maurice said and he put his underwear and clothes on.

www.ingramcontent.com/pod-product-compliance
Lightning Source LLC
Chambersburg PA
CBHW031358060726
47590CB00007B/2844